THE GREATEST OF THEM ALL

The Greatest of Them All

by

Frank Farrell

The K. S. Giniger Company, Inc.
Publishers
NEW YORK

THE GREATEST OF THEM ALL

First Published October 1982

ISBN: 0-8119-0480-6 (hardbound)
ISBN: 0-8119-0481-4 (paperback)

Distributed by

Frederick Fell Publishers, Inc.
386 Park Avenue South
New York City 10016

LIBRARY OF CONGRESS CATALOGUE CARD NUMBER: 82-83461

For MURIEL FISCHER, *my dear friend and esteemed colleague on the staff of the late New York World-Telegram & Sun, who wrote the daily society column and general features and who now writes occasional articles for The New York Times. Without her dedicated assistance in research and editing, I would never have ventured into this project.*

Contents

FOREWORD   ix

ACKNOWLEDGMENTS   xi

 1 The Living Legend   1

 2 Hello, Central . . . Hello,
    Dimension . . .   10

 3 The Hotel Never Sleeps   17

 4 From the Beginning   22

 5 A Dream Captured   39

 6 Executive Suite   52

 7 Numbers   72

 8 A Hotel within a Hotel   77

 9 And Then It Happened   91

10 Security   99

11 First and Foremost   108

12 From Kitchens to Tables   115

13 Keeping the House Clean   129

14 Keeping the Flags Flying   137

15 The Concierge Can Do It   144

16 Foreign Flavor and Favors   149

17 Lost and Found   153

18 Happy New Year, America   159

Foreword

LOWELL THOMAS

Lowell Thomas, world traveler, author, radio commentator, longtime friend and resident of The Waldorf-Astoria and president of its Marco Polo Club, wrote this foreword shortly before his death in 1981.

SOME YEARS AGO I sent my friend Frank Farrell a photograph of Lowell Jr. and myself taken with the Dalai Lama's chief advisor on a mountaintop in Lhasa, Tibet. I remember autographing the photo with: "Greetings from the Roof of the World—to Frank Farrell who is always in the center of it."

Never has there been any salutation more appropriate. For although Frank Farrell has already served his time in hell, roughing it as a frequently decorated hero of the U.S. Marines in the South Pacific and in seldom-visited areas of the Far East, I have always thought of him as a carefree, polished Mr. Midtown Manhattan.

Obviously Farrell is still in the center of this world's action and writing. He has just done a book on The Waldorf-Astoria, my favorite hotel in all the world and my home in New York City for many years. Never could there be conceivably a more fascinating subject for a book, and certainly nobody more uniquely qualified to describe the allure, the beauty of this Queen of Inns which The New York Times has crowned "the unofficial palace of New York."

Having followed his daily syndicated column, "New York—Day by Day," for more than three decades, during which he frequently wrote about The Waldorf-Astoria, Farrell has a mental warehouse full of goodies with which to entertain you.

Whether you are a native New Yorker or visitor from afar, let Farrell escort you on this entertaining ramble through The Waldorf-Astoria.

Acknowledgments

I AM MOST grateful to the following books, publications and people for the information gleaned in the research of facts, past and present, for this volume:

Be My Guest by Conrad Hilton, *Confessions of a Grand Hotel* by Horace Sutton, *Oscar of The Waldorf* by Karl Schriftgiesser, *Peacock Alley* by James Remington McCarthy, *The Silver Spade* by Whitney Bolton, *The Waldorf-Astoria Cookbook* by Ted James and Rosalind Cole, Jack O'Brian's syndicated "Voice of Broadway" column, *United Press International* article by Frederick Winship, *King Features Syndicate* article by Jim Bishop, *The Unofficial Palace* by Frank Crowninshield; other articles in The New York Times Magazine, Reader's Digest and The Saturday Evening Post; Christine Belfi, secretary to Frank G. Wangeman; John Desmond, Waldorf-Astoria security director; Jim Fayek, Waldorf Towers senior assistant manager; the late Joseph Kuhnen, retired managing director of the Bull and Bear; Thomas W. Monetti, Waldorf-Astoria director of food and beverage operations; Thomas A. Nemeth, Waldorf-Astoria director of human resources and labor relations; Beverly Schrank, secretary to Eugene R. Scanlan; and Herbert Tepper, Waldorf Towers concierge.

F.F.

THE GREATEST OF THEM ALL

The Living Legend

THE STATUE OF LIBERTY!
THE WALDORF-ASTORIA!
THE EMPIRE STATE BUILDING!
Mention any of these—and immediately almost everyone knows you are referring to New York.

But just say "Waldorf" and it will conjure up images of exquisite elegance, of grandeur and of very special individuality.

To some, it's "America's Unofficial Palace." To others, it's "America's Grand Hotel."

On the national scene, it's an adjunct of the State Department, with the Great Seal of the United States on the door of the only ambassadorial office and residence in a hotel suite anywhere in the world.

And, to the local population, it's "New York's most wonderful selling point."

In 1896, Harper's Bazaar decreed the original Waldorf was as: "The fashion of New York, the Mecca of visitors from many nations, because nowhere else in the world has any hotel come to play so important a part in the social life of a great city."

And, in 1947, The Saturday Evening Post essayed: "The average American is inclined to view The Waldorf with a certain feeling of pride, as though it were a national monument."

It's been called "a city within a city" and "a home away from home." And everything said or written about it, in song or drama, is true.

Even to the gasping exclamation of a world traveler who surveyed the grandeur of the decor and appointments, the myriad of smoothly administered services and the thousand and one comforts supplied as a matter of course to the guests: "I see it, but I don't believe it. It's not possible!"

The answer to this could only be: "Believe it! Believe it!"

Of all the accolades embracing The Waldorf-Astoria over the years, the most definitive is the personal affection with which it is regarded by the average citizen. It is a litany of enchantment, endearing and proprietary:

"My husband and I spent our wedding night at The Waldorf-Astoria," a woman in San Francisco recalls. "We vowed to spend every anniversary there. And we did for the first few years. Now we just celebrate the key anniversaries. I look forward to our thirtieth—as much for the opportunity to visit The Waldorf again, as for the fact that we've had thirty good years."

Another, from Scarsdale, remembers sentimentally: "Our first date was at The Waldorf. We met in front of the old clock in the lobby. He was late and I had memorized the inscription on the clock's bronze base by the time he arrived. And my heart was beating faster than the clock when I saw him. He doesn't know it, but whenever I'm in the city, I go back and recapture that moment, then I go home and love him all the more."

Author Jack R. Morris writes that, on one of his annual visits, he started celebrating the Yuletide season in the Bull and Bear at eleven in the morning. Between drinks, he chatted with veteran bartenders Ray and Louis until two o'clock. That's when the Christmas spirits got to him. With presents in mind, Jack ambled up to the fur shop in the main lobby. He was hell-bent on buying his wife a $17,000 mink coat and almost did.

Mrs. Morris had been waiting patiently in their room. She expected to hear from him about where to have lunch. Finally, she decided to have a look around for her missing mate. Bull and Bear bartender Ray suggested that she try the fur shop. She got there just in time to prevent Jack from blowing the family bank account.

Ad agency president Allen Falcone recalls an extremely pleasant stay in The Waldorf when he was somewhat lower on the ladder of success. He had spent three years in Germany, assigned to a branch office, and was returning to New York for a promotion to the firm's headquarters. He really couldn't afford The Waldorf that year, but he decided to live it up and create a classy impression while apartment-hunting.

Majestic Prince was Falcone's choice to win the Kentucky Derby that year. He used soap to letter the horse's name on the bathroom mirror. He printed Majestic Prince on slips of paper and taped them all over the room to remind him to place a bet on the horse.

Falcone, who is of Italian extraction, has a tanned complexion and he sported a Burt Reynolds mustache. Somehow the "news" got around the hotel that Allen was an Arab prince in disguise. And The Waldorf staff treated him like an Arab prince.

"Never had it so good," Falcone recollects. "Of course, I had to tip a little better."

P.S. Falcone remembered to place his bet—and Majestic Prince won the Derby.

Dinah Shore was not a super-star the first time she checked into The Waldorf. "But they treated me as if I were one of the top acts in the Empire Room," she recalls." I think anyone who has ever stayed there feels a loyalty to The Waldorf. The continuity is the key, and the service is very caring. I always get my favorite suite and, when I walk in, I take a deep breath and think I'm home."

A Shreveport, Louisiana, couple recount how lucky they were to get a room at The Waldorf during World War II, when the husband was on leave.

"They treated us royally, like we were a king and queen. And there were real kings and queens staying there, too. King Peter of Yugoslavia was in The Towers. I saw him. And I thought to myself: here we are, all of us under the same roof. It was like a fairy tale come true. Years passed. And one day, we were on our way to Europe and we had a waitover at Kennedy Airport. And I said to Johnny, 'Could we?' And he knew what I meant. He called a cab. We only had time for one cocktail in Peacock Alley. But, you know, it made our whole trip worthwhile."

So, what is The Waldorf-Astoria?

It is more than brick and limestone—twin crenelated towers rising 47 stories high above 81,337 square feet of the most prestigious real estate in the city.

It is more than elegant, spacious, high-ceilinged quarters—1852 rooms and suites.

It is more than deluxe banquets, commemorating gala and historic occasions, in the only two-tiered ballroom in New York.

It is more than intimate, sumptuous dining—gourmet foods and the finest vintage wines—in the seven dining rooms and lounges found on the premises.

It is more than the labyrinth of lush shops, where you can purchase designer dresses, custom-made suits, luggage, porcelains, bronzes, crested buttons, a string of pearls for $2,000, a $30,000 diamond ring, a $40 box of chocolates, or a peppermint for 25 cents. You could do all your Christmas, Easter or any time gift-shopping without ever leaving the hotel.

And it is more than velvety-cushioned sofas and upholstered chairs in the exquisite Art Deco lobby, where you can sit and read a newspaper, negotiate a contract or simply

watch the world go by. The Waldorf is a veritable museum of Art Deco studies.

It is all of these things, but so much more.

Above and beyond and most of all, The
Waldorf-Astoria is romance. For anyone who
has spent a week, a night or just a few hours
in its captivating quarters, there remains a
lifetime bond of affection. The Waldorf-
Astoria, more than any other inn in hoteldom, clutches the heart of each guest and visitor.

What it is, then, is a love affair—long and
strong, spanning the decades, in a host of rich
and enduring memories.

My friends, my colleagues and the various
people I meet, are usually politely attentive,
sometimes genuinely interested in my
project-of-the-moment. But never have I en-
countered such rhapsodic response as when I
mentioned the writing of this book.

"Oh, you will refer to Peacock Alley: Every
day was Easter Sunday and every moment a
promenade!" waxed one poetic enthusiast.

"Grandeur was sealed in its cornerstone,"
quoted another.

"Thrilling, just thrilling!" a socially elite
film star applauded. "I made my debut at the
Waldorf. Don't forget to mention the Debutante Cotillion."

"It seems to me that I attended more banquets in The Waldorf-Astoria than I had
dinners at home," a top city official jibed,
adding pensively, "The most important as-
semblages in history have been and continue
to be held there."

"Do you remember when General Motors
held its automobile shows in the Grand Ballroom of the Waldorf?" a newspaper colleague
reminded. "They delivered the cars in those
huge freight elevators."

And I still remember writing in my column
how they had to empty the gas tanks because
of fire regulations and push all those cars in.
And how the crew of carpenters transferred
that ballroom overnight into proper automo-
tive setting. It was staggering! Still is.

"Do you remember the era of the Big

Seen at The Waldorf: Mrs. Nelson Doubleday and Lena Horne (PHOTO: SAM ROSS).

Bands?" recalled a radiant prime-of-life damsel. "The superstars of entertainment were always booked into The Waldorf. Oh, the joyous nights I spent at ringside applauding Frank Sinatra, Count Basie, Peggy Lee, Victor Borge, Lena Horne in the Empire Room. And dancing to Xavier Cugat's orchestra under a blanket of stars on the Starlight Roof! I can still smell the gardenias I wore at my school prom."

I shall always flinch at the fleeting recollection of a hot Friday night in June when I was budding out of my teens. No school Saturday. Prom week. A time to howl. There were eight of us at that beautiful girl's graduation party. The fellows wore white evening jackets with black tux trousers and black bows. The four debs with us were all in white gowns. We had a ringside table only a few feet from maestro Eddie Lane and his orchestra, all attired in white jackets. The party setting was perfect—except for Prohibition.

Legally, alcoholic beverages were unobtainable, but my Uncle Bill was a deputy commissioner of police. He seemed to know all about the 18th Amendment and how to cope with it. Uncle Bill had one of the finest wine and booze cellars in New York City. Therefore I implored him to give me something to enhance our Waldorf party. He dredged up a magnum of sparkling Burgundy. I have ever since suspected that Uncle Bill had a wry sense of humor. He neglected to warn me that sparkling Burgundy must be thoroughly chilled before uncorking.

Inside my jacket, I smuggled the magnum into The Waldorf at body heat and hid it under our table. Then I flamboyantly ordered "setups for eight." The waiter brought the usual highball glasses containing ice cubes.

Everyone at the table sat admiringly as I secured the giant bottle on the chair between my legs, removed the foil and proceeded to unscrew the wiring that fastened the cork to the magnum.

Then came the explosion. The cork shot up to the ceiling. The rich red wine erupted like Mount St. Helens, mushroomed in midair like an A-bomb and the fallout crimsoned the white raiment of all and sundry in the immediate vicinity, including Eddie Lane's crew. The musicians reacted to the shower with an offbeat clinker that embarrassingly called everyone's attention to Farrell's Folly.

"Oh, well," I philosophized at the age of 20, as my party of eight beat a hasty disorderly retreat from the hotel, "you can't win 'em all!"

So it goes. The anecdotes. The memories. The personal recollections.

If, in the overall, The Waldorf-Astoria means something special to every man and woman, young and old, who has visited it, then this book is truly meant for each of them.

For this is my Valentine to my favorite hotel, the one Conrad Hilton dubbed long before he made it the crown jewel of his vast system, "The greatest of them all!"

For him, for myself, for all of us, I give you The Waldorf-Astoria, a living legend of our times, past, present and future.

OVERLEAF: New York's newspaper columnists may spend more time at The Waldorf than they do at home. COUNTERCLOCKWISE: syndicated columnist Jack O'Brian is heard daily on New York radio station WOR; Bert Bachrach is also nationally syndicated; veteran columnist Louis Sobol is with Jerome Zipkin, a number one subject for columnists; Cindy Adams and husband Joey Adams write columns for the Post; and, as "Suzy," Aileen Mehle is society columnist for The New York Daily News; nationally-syndicated Post columnist Earl Wilson and his "B.W." Rosemary, are always there if something important is happening; James Brady's "Page Six" in The New York Post is widely read and he appears on CBS television; and Liz Smith writes for The Daily News and is seen on Channel 4 (PHOTO: MATTHEW MAURO).

7

Hello, Central . . .
Hello, Dimension . . .

A WOMAN IN BROOKLYN confesses a now-cured compulsion to call The Waldorf-Astoria each morning just to inquire the time.

"I could have gotten it from the clock or radio," she admits. "But calling The Waldorf gave me a rich feeling. It was a nice way to start the day."

Nor did the erudite gentleman from Boston flinch at the response to his request to speak to "The king, please."

"Which king, sir?" the hotel operator asked. "We seem to have several in the house today."

Both stories are true. And rank among the most retold tales of life in the telephone post of The Waldorf-Astoria.

The system, it is said, could service a city of 25,000, comparable to Dover, Delaware, or Helena, Montana.

But the source and variety of Waldorf calls and callers make it vastly different.

Where else, for instance, are the operators besieged by long-distance pleas for recipes? ("Mostly, it's The Waldorf salad. Sometimes we transfer the call to the chef, sometimes we just recite the ingredients. By now, we know it by heart.")

And where else would a member of the royal house of Belgium place a call from the coast, just to chat with a hotel operator? (It was old King Albert, obviously taken with The Waldorf's telephonic efficiency and courtesy, who rang up from San Francisco while on a nationwide tour. "Just wanted to say, Hello!"

And where else would a longtime hotel resident make a personal visit to the telephone room because she "always wondered about the face behind the voice"? (It was Mrs. Douglas MacArthur, who asked The Towers bell captain to escort her. "I just wanted to see what you all looked like," she confessed, "and how all of this works.")

To the one-and-a-half-million callers who annually dial 355-3000 (Area Code 212) for reservations, information and person-to-person, The Waldorf operators are not only faceless, they are nameless.

What seems like a pencil mark on Marian Jeffries' right cheek is her almost invisible microphone. She is The Waldorf's director of telecommunications and is seen with operator Ruth Jones at their work stations (PHOTO: BILL MARK).

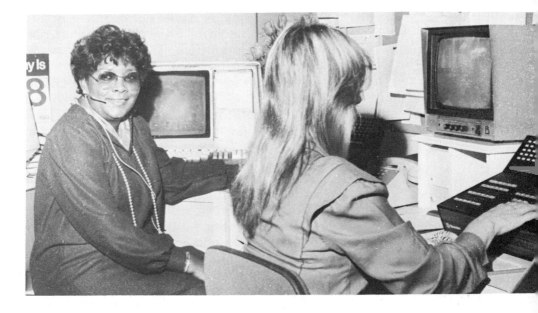

Identification is by number only. "Waldorf-Astoria, good morning, Operator 30. May I help you?" the greeting goes. And for someone who urges, "You've been so nice, please tell me your name," the reply is always the same: "I'm sorry, we are not allowed to give out that information."

Today, the telephone room, located on the second floor—not far from its sister Room Service operation—is a gleaming replica of a space command post.

The operators wear Star Trek headgear and sit in plush swivel chairs at long low desks in front of electronic consoles. As calls come in, they push buttons which produce images on their computer screen. One button shows what rooms are available; another reveals the number of occupants in room, where they are from, when they checked in, the expected date of departure and whether or not they wish to receive calls.

Two operators do nothing but take messages. Each message is transmitted verbally (every guest phone has a red light flashing to denote "message waiting") and also typed for room delivery (in a variety of languages).

"It's double work, but effective," supervisor Marian Jeffries declares.

The main focus of the command post is a robot-like machine adjacent to the supervisor's glassed office. It's name is "Audichron" and it is programmed to respond to seven hundred wake-up requests simultaneously.

The prerecorded announcements run something like this: "Good morning, Waldorf time is 7:01. Current temperature is six degrees." ("That one really gets them up," an operator laughs.)

The Audichron never ceases to amaze the oldtimers, who can still remember when The Waldorf's number was more melodically pronounced "Eldorado 5-3000"—and the wake-ups posed a herculean hurdle for the relay team responsible for ringing hundreds of rooms at precisely 7 a.m.

"In the old system, the girls had to set up

each position for the morning wake-ups at 4 a.m. We could not possibly hit the 7 a.m. target for, say, two hundred (to four hundred rooms. So we'd start ten or fifteen minutes earlier, end ten minutes after. Either way, there were rumblings."

Still, there was a tremendous sense of accomplishment when the last 7 a.m. wake-up was spiked and the race began for the 7:30 a.m. calls and so on.

"It was more demanding, but more dramatic. The big switchboard, the different color plugs—each one had a certain meaning.

"And callers were more relaxed then. They would talk at greater length. It's more businesslike today."

However, progress must be accepted. And, in a sense, *"Dimension* 2000," installed in November 1979, has eased the physical strain upon the telephone operators.

Operator 13, a Waldorf "Hello" for 26 years, vividly recalls the frenetic pace of plugging in on the old multiple switchboard.

"We sat on high stools with heavy headsets, and the board was so big that in order to ring 42A, way up on top, we had to stand up . . .

"It was hard on the back and the shoulders and arms. I had sore wings. The wings, the wings," she gestured, pressing her elbows in, "they used to ache after a long day. And the headset weighed heavily . . ."

Some things never change. The old-time teasing, "Hello, Central . . ." refrain. (Today "Hello Dimension," would be more apropos.) And the requests for recipes. ("Mostly, The Waldorf salad or macaroon . . .") Even calls asking for advice on preparing a buffet for twenty-five. ("The caller was from Elmyra, Ohio, and she was connected to the chef's office.")

Travel may be swifter, conversations shorter and guests may now dial long distance direct. But the telephone credo has never altered: "Courtesy, politeness, helpfulness at all times—for the royalty in the Towers or the convention guest in the main house."

One convention threw the phone headquarters into a tizzy. While they added a decidedly decorative note as they ambled through the lobby, the hundreds of models who convened for a fashion show and banquet the summer of 1981, cast telecommunications into a dither.

"There were so many requests we had to keep on file: 'If B.R. calls, I'm out; if J.S. calls, I'm visiting Room 1120 . . .'"

It was a jigsaw puzzle of sorts. But the phone center managed to cope, albeit all breathed a uniform sigh of relief when the lively, leggy group departed.

There is, in fact, very little the capable crew doesn't take in stride. After all, they speak daily with the most famous and important people in the world. And they handle affairs-of-state with the aplomb of a diplomat, even to the correct pronunciation of oft-confounding surnames.

Every afternoon, the supervisor scans the daily events sheet for the following day, snipping the arrivals list which she will Xerox for all 32 operators on the three-shift 24-hours schedule.

It's a particularly lengthy and tongue-twisting roster when the United Nations is in session and foreign ministers and other foreign officials descend *en masse* upon the security haven of The Towers.

One late September afternoon forecast the arrival of missions from Somali, Indonesia, Syria, Thailand, the United Arab Emirates, Iraq, Saudi Arabia, Japan and Mali.

"Sixteen rooms for Saudi Arabia!" Operator 13 whistled. "Well, we know where the action is. Her eye pinpointed the last entry on the list. "Mali? Where's Mali?" She consulted a handy directory. "They keep adding new countries," she moaned.

The daily events sheet also specified which flags will be hoisted the next day. "People keep calling up and asking: 'What flags are flying today?' And we can't very well see from where we sit."

Their second floor window overlooks Lexington Avenue, a more placid perch than their previous quarters facing 50th Street.

"I remember hanging out of the window when Khrushchev and Castro were here. It was bedlam! Security all around the hotel, armed guards at The Towers, the lineup of motorcycles at right angles on the whole street, from Park to Lexington."

In a way, great moments of history were recorded at The Waldorf-Astoria switchboard.

When the MacArthurs arrived from Tokyo, after the General was recalled by Truman, The Waldorf board was swamped. "We just had lights burning . . . The number was impossible to reach . . . The messages were stacked in piles!"

It echoed the arrival of the Duke and Duchess of Windsor, just after their historic abdication and marriage. For that occasion, The Waldorf had to install a switchboard and an operator right in the ducal suite.

Then British Prime Minister Harold Macmillan and then Soviet leader Nikita Khrushchev talk at The Waldorf Towers (PHOTO: WILL WEISSBERG).

15

In the Dimension 2000 era, the Democratic Convention of 1980 was a night to reckon with. "Senator Kennedy was staying here and, when he lost the nomination [*to President Jimmy Carter*], we got calls from all over the country. Mostly, people crying and begging, please, could they talk to him . . . And the messages! 'Just tell him I love him!' . . . It makes you wonder what would have happened had he won."

Known for its innovations, while strongly maintaining tradition, The Waldorf was the first hotel to hire male telephone operators.

"They are perfect for the night shift," the supervisor mused. "It seems to fit in fine with their daytime schedules." (One, for instance, keeps his vocal chords in tune on the telephone from midnight to dawn, then scoots around to his theater auditions.)

And the telephone room is as adjunt to The Waldorf's intense security watch. "Our wake-ups are programmed to ring a room three times if the first call isn't picked up. If there's no answer, the call is repeated five minutes later and five minutes after that. If still no answer, it shows on the printout, and we get an alarm on our console: 'Room 1701 does not answer.' So we notify security to check on the occupant, to make sure everything is all right."

The role of the chief operator has come a long way, even in title. "We are now, officially, director of telecommunications," Mrs. Jeffries grins.

But the basic premise of the department remains, as always, and emphatically: "The telephone is the first line of communication to The Waldorf. I tell my operators: Your voice and your manner reflect the policy and manner of this hotel. It's got to be better than good. It's got to be grand."

And it always is, whatever the time of day—or night. . .

The Hotel Never Sleeps

BETWEEN THE HOURS OF midnight and dawn an aura of peach blankets The Waldorf-Astoria. Or so it seems to the somnolent guest.

Actually, crews of employees on the graveyard shift bustle as briskly in the care and repair of the hotel's backstage regions as their counterparts do by day.

Telephone calls, due to time differences, are nonstop between New York and London, Tokyo, Cairo, Sydney, Buenos Aires, Johannesburg and elsewhere around the clock.

And the lobby, albeit draped in tranquility, can be abruptly aroused by a jolt of nocturnal lightning.

This was vividly brought home to me by an incident involving a dear and departed confrere.

If my friend, Duncan McMartin, were not the very epitome of the playboy of the western world, it was not for lack of trying.

Fortunately, most of his merry andrew

antics were rarely indulged in his home away from home—which happened to be The Waldorf Towers.

At the hotel, employees only knew him as a powerfully built athletic gentleman, with a roguish sense of humor, who always tipped most generously. All of which paid off for him one eventful night.

Duncan's father had discovered gold in Canada and pioneered a fabulous mine when Duncan was in rompers. This left young McMartin with a big problem after his dad passed away: How to spend $10,000 a week to keep abreast of the interest on the bundle he inherited? (In those days, subway slots took nickels.)

Duncan thought nothing of phoning a favorite barber in Beverly Hills and commandeering him to fly to New York because he "hadn't enjoyed a decent shave in weeks."

One sizzling summer night in Manhattan, Duncan was cooling off in a midtown oasis. He fanned himself with a few highballs, then decided to take a breezy spin in his new Rolls Royce convertible, which he had parked outside at Madison Avenue and 52nd Street with the top down.

He jauntily leaped into the driver's seat, gripped the wheel, and pushed down on the gas pedal. The car whizzed north on Madison Avenue.

It was 2:30 a.m. There was little traffic. The night air was soothing. His "air-conditioning" accelerated with the speed of the car from 50 to 60 miles an hour. Suddenly, the traffic signal switched from green to yellow and the driver in front applied his brakes. Duncan, too, hit the brake pedal with all the force of his 210-pound frame.

Too late. The Rolls plowed into the jalopy. The driver of the struck car piled out yelling "Whiplash!" and "Police!" with embarassing volume.

Duncan wanted no part of police, jail or a lawsuit, each one inviting undesirable publicity. He eyed the crumpled steel he had created; and, on the spot, offered to buy the man "a brand new car." Suddenly, there was silence. Together, they pushed their damaged vehicles to the curbside and proceeded by taxi to The Waldorf.

On the way, the "injured party" made some mental calculations. The owner of a Rolls convertible, residing at The Waldorf, could definitely afford $5,000. (A more realistic settlement would have been $500.) Duncan did not demur. He simply did not have it on him or at hand.

At the hotel, the night cashier sighed over Duncan's dilemma, and explained there wasn't that much in the till in the wee hours. He could manage a loan of $3,000. . .

So Duncan buttonholed the bellman. Could he pass the hat among the night crew—and whatever they chipped in as a loan would be doubled on its return the following night. The additional $2,000 ransom was readily raised.

For the playboy, it was just another chaotic episode in a full and flamboyant career. And for the people who toiled between midnight and morn at the celebrated inn, it was just another chapter in a series of full and stimulating nights to remember.

After all, when you are an important cog in the wheel of the most famous hotel in the most famous metropolis in the world, you're groomed for perpetual motion.

In a way, The Waldorf-Astoria is a city within itself. And like a city, The Waldorf never sleeps.

All through the night, telephone operators are on duty at the consoles. There's a room clerk at the reservations desk. Elevators are running. Watchmen and security officers quietly make their rounds.

Far below the lobby level, in the subbasement regions, engineers are at work in the boiler room, electricians are checking the power plant, maintaining the machinery that provides a hot shower, a glass of ice water, steam in the laundry, frost in the freezer, heat in winter, air-conditioning in summer—and a light to read this book by.

Elsewhere, in the dark hours, cleaners are

scrubbing tile kitchens, waxers are buffing ballroom floors. Housemen and maids are vacuuming and dusting, airing and preparing rooms for the new day.

At dawn, trucks from farms and mills, piers and markets draw up to the hotel's platforms and unload their wares. Sometimes it's a hundred trucks a day.

Chickens by the carload, meat by the ton, truckloads of potatoes, crates of asparagus, sacks of flour, sugar and spice. Frog's legs from Honolulu, melons from Spain, crab meat from Seattle, pineapples from the Azores, chops from New Jersey, duckling from Long Island, coffee from Colombia, lobsters from Maine.

Every item is checked and carefully weighed. ("You've got to watch for the short weights. It's maybe thirty-five cents off here, a half-dollar there, but, in the day's billing, the pennies saved can multiply to thousands of dollars.") Overhead costs are so stupendous that management is challenged to its elastic limits and ever alert on how to control and reduce any conceivable fraction of mistake or waste.

Long before the guests arise, the kitchen is geared to serve the thousand-and-one calls for "room service" and its breakfast specials plus assorted *a la cartes* all day. One man makes a salad, another stirs the soup; one man cooks omelettes, another slices fruit; one carves a turkey, another stuffs tomatoes; one whips up pastry, another fries potatoes. All through the morning, the momentum mounts, each station manned in the preparation of menus for noon luncheons, dinner banquets and meals for all the restaurants.

Meanwhile, floors above, the housekeeping department has unlocked its vast shelves of bed sheets and pillowcases, blankets and towels, washcloths and tissues. Also dusters and sweepers, mops and brushes, soap and detergents—bins of supplies costing millions of dollars per year.

Every day is spring cleaning at The Waldorf-Astoria. It begins with the stripping of a bed. ("If the bed isn't made right, nothing else seems right.")

And, too, the furniture must be clear of dust, the mirror free from smudge; no rings around the bathtub or sink, nor fingerprints on doorknobs or drawers.

Housemen on the rounds carry off a sofa's sagging cushion or a stained armchair for recovering and repair in the upholstery shop upstairs.

Elsewhere, a frayed shade or a worn blind is restrung and rehung. And a wing of rooms is marked "out of order" while painters and plasterers, polishers and carpenters redo like new.

All the while, in the lobby, guests are checking in and checking out. It's a veritable merry-go-round of baggage and bellmen. With a system of sorts: a bellman at the entrance, another at the desk, another near the newsstand—and one at every pillar and post.

In the background, the front office hums with its computers and calculators, confirming reservations, acknowledging special requests, bookkeeping and billing, accounting and auditing, recording charges, checking credits—and politely heeding complaints.

At two minutes to noon, a meeting ends and the room empties. For the gathering, the business of the day is over. But for the meeting room, it's business as usual—only of a different kind.

Quickly, chairs are stacked four-high, tables are rolled in. In precision drill, table legs are unfolded, tabletops set with cloth, china, glassware, cutlery, candlesticks, numbers and napkins—and a roll on every plate.

Industrial slogans are moved out, flowers moved in; the room is ready for a luncheon.

Finally, when the last reveler has left for home, the last guest bedded down for the night, a quiescent peace settles over the hotel. It seems steeped in slumber, so silent and still.

And yet, an operator is at the console, an elevator is running, a vacuum is droning, and they're tinkering in the boiler room again.

From the Beginning

TODAY'S WALDORF-ASTORIA is some kind of
dream come true for me. Because I was there
for the groundbreaking. And I spent my boyhood Saturdays watching it take shape on
Park Avenue. Every weekend, whatever and
wherever my job, I would find the time—in
the morning, at lunch or after work—to scoot
to the site and stand with the other gaping
sidewalk superintendents.

I watched the skeleton on stilts fill in and
grow wider and taller, until the copper-plated
turrets dominated all they surveyed for miles
around.

The Waldorf-Astoria rose like a Taj Mahal
out of the ashes and blur of the Great Depression, a classic of beauty and perfection and a
joy to all who stood awesomely in its rays of
splendor.

It was a symbol of shining American re-
sourcefulness, imagination, courage and de-
termination in the wake of the nation's worst
reverses.

And, when it was completed, in the blight of October, 1931, the hurrahs resounded around the world.

There were, to be sure, the doubting Thomases, those who shook their heads in disbelief at all that gilt and wondered pessimistically if it could survive.

And while there was no champagne to toast its inception—Prohibition decreed a dry christening—some thousands of bottles of bubbly were consumed in gold-rimmed crystal salutes for its fiftieth anniversary champagne reception on September 30, 1981.

Many of the more than 2,500 persons who visited the tinselled Grand Ballroom for the mammoth golden anniversary had likewise attended the 1931 baptism. And there were a score or more who recalled the final rites at the old site on Fifth Avenue and 34th Street, where the Empire State Building stands now.

For The Waldorf-Astoria we know today—a half-century structure of magnificent Art Deco decor, haute cuisine and elegant but earthy hospitality—is really a rebirth of the original Waldorf-Astoria which sparkled almost ninety years ago.

If we were to script The Waldorf's birth and growth, it would read like a fairy tale in two parts, The Old and The New. And it begins: Once upon a time, in 1890, there were three wise men of vision and their names were Astor, Bartlett and Boldt. . .

William Waldorf Astor was the first to think of building a luxury high-rise hotel on Fifth Avenue. He had the money to do it, and the location—the site of his family mansion.

Abner Bartlett was the man with a fantasy as to what this unique hotel would look like, feel like, ultimately be. . . In business parlance, he was to become "executive vice-president and chief operating officer" for the William Waldorf Astor enterprise.

George C. Boldt was already established as a guiding genius among the nation's innkeepers. He was then director of Philadelphia's celebrated Bellevue Hotel.

At the time, the only hotels in the city (or

the nation, for that matter) were mostly commercial, catering to transients. Comparable to today's motels, born of necessity, there was a chain-store sameness about them, with the rudimentary furniture and closets and little more.

That was not what the Astor-Bartlett-Boldt triumvirate had in mind. That is why they called in architect Henry J. Hardenbergh to explain their vision of a large, luxurious hotel with homelike ambiance and ample dining rooms, ballrooms and other public spaces.

Could Hardenbergh conceive a sort of castle for the traveling elite, an hospitable hostelry that could also lavishly cater to social gatherings? For in that era of changing patterns, the social milieu was evidently sprouting new directions, with many elite families moving out of their grand mansions into smaller townhouses. And where would they entertain?

As home entertainment dwindled, so would the great personal chefs. People would be seeking refined divertissement, along with epicurean fare. Why not combine them in the elegant environs of a grand hotel?

So went the muses' conception of the original Waldorf.

Why the name "Waldorf"? Because that was the tag of the little village in Germany where the Astors originated.

And so the architect Hardenbergh joined the three wise men in the blueprint creation of superlative edifices and interiors that would set the stage for innkeepers of the future.

Plans for the original Waldorf were filed in the autumn of 1890.

Amid great curiosity (and some minor grumblings), the first of the twin Astor mansions of Fifth Avenue, between 33rd and 34th Streets, came tumbling down. And the dazzling steel frame for the revolutionary Waldorf Hotel began its dramatic ascension in the summer of 1891.

It was to be seven stories high. But Mr.

Architect's drawing showing difference in size between old and new Waldorfs.

Boldt considered "13" a lucky number; so they added six more floors. It now ranked as a skyscraper and was hailed as such at its world premiere on the 13th of March, 1893.

Less than two years later, the second mansion, belonging to cousin John Jacob Astor IV, was demolished. And up went the 17-story Astoria in November, 1897.

The twin hotels were joined by a corridor—and a double hyphen—both of which were to attain a distinction that lasted ever after.

In that era of elegance, ladies wore hats with plumes. And as they strolled the length of the corridor connecting the hotels, they looked like peacocks on parade.

It was a society editor of The New York

Herald who viewed the plumed procession and promptly dubbed the walkway "Peacock Alley" "The appellation stuck and so did the custom. "Peacock Alley"became the gathering place for those who made fashion, those who reported fashion and those who came to ogle and comment.

It was said that, upon arrival, guests would check into their rooms, take a bath (a commodious attraction of the luxury hotel), then put on their best and strut from the lobby through Peacock Alley into the Palm Room where they would dine leisurely and well— with a great display of champagne buckets.

This was also the era when a new breed of wealth were elbowing the founding families of the "four hundred" and vintaged aristocracy out of their entrenched social positions.

They had to be taught the proper foods to eat, the proper wines to drink. And they learned it befittingly at the old Waldorf. The Waldorf also instilled culture in the nouveau riche, with the customary pomp and circumstance.

The opening night ball featured a concert by the New York Philharmonic Orchestra under the direction of Walter Damrosch.

Mrs. William K. Vanderbilt underwrote the expenses of the festive charity event benefitting the St. Mary's Free Hospital for Children. The prudently selective guest list lured prominent families from the Social Registers of New York, Philadelphia, Boston and Baltimore, who came dressed in their finest— despite the buckets of rain—at the bidding of the acknowledged arbiter of New York society.

The combination of the Vanderbilt "command" invitation and the Philharmonic performance was all that was needed to establish the new hotel as a reservoir of culture and entertainment. And it soon became the accepted gathering place for the so-called Four Hundred.

It is interesting to note how the term "the Four Hundred" evolved. *The* Mrs. Astor (Mrs. William Backhouse Astor) was planning an elaborate farewell shindig before she left these shores to take up permanent residence in England. She presented her social advisor, Ward McAlister, with a guest list of many hundred. McAlister frowned at the thought of the Astor ballroom packed with wall-to-wall people. He informed the *grande dame* there was really only room enough to accommodate four hundred comfortably. She left it to him to whittle down the numbers. In pruning the list, McAlister thus arbitrarily dictated who ranked as the indisputable first (400) families of New York society.

The listing may have ruffled some feathers; but it intrigued the newspapers who leaped upon the number in print and commentary. An expression was coined. "McAlister's Four Hundred" became the foundation for the *Social Register*.

The atmosphere was ripe for The Waldorf to reign as the place to rest, reside, dine, entertain and to see and be seen. Moreover, it had an eminent major domo expertly skilled in meeting and greeting the flock who wandered through its heralded halls.

Oscar Tschirky held that title and imbued it with such style, zest and eclat that, from the day of his arrival (he was the first employee hired) until his retirement, he and The Waldorf were inextricably intertwined.

Oscar applied for the job before the hotel was completed. He was already *maitre d'* at Delmonico's fashionable restaurant. And George Boldt requested letters of reference, the indomitable Oscar delivered only one— ten pages of autographed testimonials from leading dignitaries of the day, among them George Gould, Diamond Jim Brady, Lillian Russell and Richard Harding Davis.

Oscar was a greeter par excellence. However, contrary to popular belief, he was never a chef. That he came to be regarded as *the* authority on gourmet cuisine, the oracle of American gastronomy, was because he taught a slew of new American millionaires to eat in French.

As Waldorf host supreme, he unraveled the

mysteries of the haute cuisine menu and educated plebian palates to such delicacies as French sauces, dressings, pastries and wines.

So Oscar was no chef ("My wife would never even allow me in the kitchen"), but he was a connoisseur. And when he presided over a salad bowl or chafing dish, he was the very essence of showmanship—enough to ensure his niche forever in the storehouse of Waldorf legends.

It is ironic, too, that he would be so glorified by his first name only by thousands who never knew (nor would they be able to pronounce) his surname.

The story is told of the time Oscar's wife called and asked for "Mr. Tschirky." He was paged in all the usual places. But he never answered the page. He had, he admitted ruefully, forgotten his own last name.

On the occasion of his fiftieth wedding anniversary in 1937, a group of sixteen organizations tendered him a banquet attended by 1200 people. Congratulatory messages came from President Franklin Roosevelt, his entire cabinet and officials of all levels and lands.

Oscar checked over details in the morning and at six p.m. put on his dinner jacket, then inspected each party held in the hotel that night, toured each public restaurant and finally responded to a messenger dispatched by the committee on arrangements to remind him to escort his wife to dinner.

It is fair to say that Oscar and The Waldorf were wedded. And each enhanced the image of the other.

But what really sparked The Waldorf's fame, echoing its name throughout the world, were the royal luminaries who adopted the hotel from the very beginning.

Spain's delegation to Chicago's World Fair of 1893, headed by the Duke and Duchess of Veragua, were among the first distinguished visitors from overseas to register for a royal suite (with canopied bed upon a dais, tapestries and regal appointments).

Japan's Marquis Yamagata was next, in 1896, a rather conventional visit.

The most spectacular—to mark The Waldorf as VIP headquarters for all time—was the ceremonial signing-in of Mr. Li, globally identified as Li Hung-Chang, Viceroy of the Empire of China, when he arrived a few months later in 1896.

His other titles were Prime Minister, Minister of Foreign Affairs, Senior Guardian of his country's ruler, Earl of Suh Chi and Commander of China's Northern Army.

He arrived on an American ship, debarking at a Fulton Street downtown dock with what appeared to be an entire oriental regiment. He was borne ashore in a sedan chair and his Chinese New Year parade uptown was embellished with exploding firecrackers, reverberating rockets and the gawking exclamations of a million onlookers. New York's population already had its share of Chinese (almost as numerous as San Francisco's); but New Yorkers had never previously been exposed to a genuine Far Eastern nobleman.

The slender, diminutive, exotically garbed Mr. Li seemed like someone out of an ancient Chinese fable as he and his coterie of minor royalty, aides, lackeys, cooks and bakers—bearing stoves, woks and other native impedimenta, including rickshaws—wended their way along the confettied parade route to The Waldorf's front desk.

Elaborate arrangements had been made. But Oscar fretted over Mr. Li's refusal to taste any of the hotel's special culinary creations. All of the Viceroy's meals were prepared by his chefs and the Imperial One even had his own Chinese dishes at the banquet in his honor. His demeanor remained inscrutable, while Oscar's grew increasingly glum.

However, when Oscar brought his children to the royal suite, the atmosphere instantly changed. Mr. Li's countenance was wreathed in smiles as he greeted and patted the enthralled youngsters. He talked with them at length via an interpreter. And proud father Oscar, in the wink of an eye, became the Viceroy's number one admirer.

The worldwide press coverage of Mr. Li's

On May 1, 1929, the last day the Waldorf-Astoria occupied its site on Fifth Avenue between 33rd and 34th Streets, one final grand party was held in the magnificent ballroom decked with trailing arbutus and magnolia blossoms. In memory of our shared past on what was in 1799 the John Thomson farm, the Empire State Building is delighted to present these flowers for the "new" Waldorf-Astoria's 50th Anniversary, with our heartiest congratulations. Little did the New York Times know in 1929, when it editorially wondered whether there actually would be another Waldorf-Astoria built, commenting that after all, the era that made the hotel famous had passed into oblivion. But in 1981, as both the Waldorf-Astoria and the Empire State Building celebrate golden jubilees, we can only conclude that... being born on the Thomson farm was lucky for both of us!

The owners of the Empire State Building, erected on the site of the old Waldorf, salute the new Waldorf on its golden jubilee.

sensational visit served as a magnet for cosmopolites of every rank and nation. Reservation requests poured in from all over the globe.

There was another facet of the hotel that had a magnetic lure. All Europe envied America its most famous innovation—the bath. And The Waldorf plumbing—"Hot water in every room!"—was a curiosity among some visitors from abroad.

When Prince Henry of Prussia (brother of Kaiser Wilhelm of Germany) arrived in 1902, advance word reached The Waldorf that the Prince was most anxious to inspect the plumbing of which he had heard so much. Well, it just so happened that at the vital hour when the Prince was being piped ashore, the plumbing in the royal suite went on the blink. In its finest moment of diplomacy, management tactfully escorted the Prince on a tour of Peacock Alley.

While they tarried there, frantic plumbers raced from the boiler room to the royal suite and back. One last twist of a Stillson wrench and steaming hot water came flooding into the tub. The last overalled figure skittered out of the back door just as His Royal Highness walked in the front and asked, on cue, might he, please, be shown "the wonderful plumbing. . ."

But, among innkeepers, the reputation of this ideal hostelry rested on the shoulders of its august proprietor, George C. Boldt. The Danish immigrant was regarded as a sort of Moses the Lawgiver to the hotel business. And, when Boldt died, in the Christmas frost of 1916, the entire industry mourned his passing. His death had a stunning effect on the landmark corner of Fifth Avenue and 34th Street.

For three years—although World War I kept the hotel busy and prosperous—there was a noticeable gap in vibrant leadership. Into this vacuum, in 1919, stepped an inspirational figure, General (later Senator) Coleman Du Pont, whose preliminary feat ws to "capture" one Lucius Messenger Boomer.

Boomer had attained the acknowledged position of "Hotelman of the Year" when Du Pont approached him with an offer he could not refuse: "I will take over the Waldorf, if you will run it."

Thus was created the Boomer-Du Pont Properties Corporation, which purchased The Waldorf-Astoria name, its lease and its contents. (But not the ground under the hotel. That was still owned jointly by William Waldorf Astor and the estate of John Jacob Astor IV.)

World War I was scarcely etched into history when America was seized by zealous evangelists who zeroed in on alcoholic consumption as the source of all evil. In one tailspin of psychological guilt, following the tradition of Carrie Nation, John Barleycorn cartoons and a trail of tear-drenched mothers and wives, the Eighteenth Amendment to the Constitution became the law of the land, in statute if not in practice.

With Prohibition, the nation went dry. And bootlegging became the underworld handmaiden to those who pursued booze at any cost. In the wake of Prohibition, many fine hotels and restaurants, clubs and other social centers fell as if stricken by a plague. And in their stead, speakeasies—peekaboo panelled hideaways, run or controlled by mobsters—sprang up like weeds, plying unlicensed liquor with the offbeat entertainment at outrageous prices. But thirsty patrons beat a path to their doors.

Coupled with the changing social mores was the gradual decline of domestic help and the consequent trend of wealthy families to forsake their large downtown mansions for upper East Side town houses and apartments.

The Waldorf-Astoria saw the handwriting on the wall. It was just a matter of time before it, too, became outdated. In December, 1928, announcement was made that the hotel would be torn down and replaced by an office building. On May 3, 1929, the management locked up and moved out.

The closing event was called "Employees'

Day" because every penny spent in the hotel that day went into a fund for those who had served so faithfully and well over the years.

Then came a clean sweep of The Waldorf's contents, much coveted by collectors and souvenir hunters. Then the wreckers and then the construction workers for the cloud-piercing Empire State Building.

The only thing that remained was The Waldorf-Astoria name. That was retained by Lucius Boomer, a token bequeathed him by a grateful board of directors for the sum of one dollar.

Boomer went South—into retirement. He had hardly dug his toes into the Florida sands when an urgent telephone call beckoned him back north. A group of New York financiers, lamenting the loss of their homing grounds, were prepared to build a new Waldorf-Astoria—if Boomer would give them permission to use the name and agree to manage the new hotel.

Once again, it was an offer he could not refuse.

Investment firms like Hayden Stone, Hallgarten, Baker Weeks eagerly subscribed. Backers of the project bought and sold $11,000,000 in bonds and some of the stock. The New York Central and the New York, New Haven and Hartford railroads put up $10,000,000 and supplied the site, one of the most valuable city blocks in the world, on Park Avenue, a short distance north of the Grand Central Terminal. Twenty-one bankers and financiers invested $7,000,000 in Waldorf stock. They put up their money on October 28, 1929. The next day, the stock market crashed.

In spite of the gloomy business prospects and the glut of new hotels in New York, the contractors went bravely ahead. After all, they were not merely building a hotel. They were building another Waldorf! And they went about it as a labor of love. They were courageous optimists who believed the Great Depression would be of short duration.

The top-drawer architectural firm of

Schultze and Weaver sketched the inspiring blueprints for Thompson-Starrett in the physical fruition of the sumptuous new Waldorf-Astoria.

Every piece of hardware that went into the hotel—doorknobs, window fittings, cabinets—was specially designed. The bathtubs were custom-built and the bathroom fixtures were specially made of nickel silver. Entire rooms from old English manor houses were brought over and reconstructed into The Waldorf.

Throughout the construction period the publicity build-up for the new Waldorf was tremendous. Lucius Boomer, who had moved his family into a cop-op apartment at 300 Park Avenue (an address shared by the famous Sherry's) so he could keep an eye on the progress of the steel and concrete tabernacle at 301 Park Avenue, across the street, was not unaware of the practical dividends from good publicity. He hired a Canadian master of the art, a fellow named Ted Saucier.

But it was the blue-ribbon combination of Boomer and Oscar who imbued the project with their impeccable standards of perfection. And they were aided and abetted by the sterling talents of Ted Saucier in perpetuating the gilded image of the old Waldorf-Astoria into the new.

Saucier was a sorcerer at whetting the public's appetite for The Waldorf's debut. And he was insatiable in his avidity for keeping the hotel's name in print. For twenty years, the astute public relations director maintained a status enviable to all others of his genre. It was not for naught that he won the hard-earned respect of hard-nosed newsmen like myself.

Prior to the opening of the new Waldorf, Saucier, behind the scenes, engineered (and anonymously co-authored) a book called *Peacock Alley*, which recorded the life and times, facts and lore of the old Waldorf. Its publication provided a sentimental prelude to the premiere of the new Waldorf-Astoria.

As opening day neared, Saucier blitzed the newsrooms with day-by-day bulletins. They reached a crescendo when traffic on Park Avenue was stopped to allow fifty rug-layers to manipulate the new lobby carpet into the front entrance. (It was pointed out that it was the largest hand-tufted carpet ever made; thirty rugmakers in Czechoslovakia had labored ten months tying 12,600,000 knots into a languid Persian-garden scene.)

At last the climactic day arrived—October 1, 1931. I was there—along with tens of thousands of others—who queued up for hours awaiting a turn to rubberneck inside.

It was a grand occasion, resembling the dedication of some great public memorial. Leaders of New York's cultural, social, business and political life were on hand. Orchestras played in the galleries. A banquet was held in the Grand Ballroom. Twenty-five thousand people came to see and to marvel.

Oscar stood at the head of the stairs, just as he stationed himself at the entrance of the old Waldorf on opening day thirty-eight years before.

And the President of the United States delivered a message of congratulations, received by The Waldorf's own master antenna and broadcast nationally. A hush fell over the assemblage as Herbert Hoover, standing in the Cabinet Room of the White House at dusk in the depth of the Depression spoke into an NBC microphone: "The erection of this great structure has been . . . an exhibition of courage and confidence to the whole nation."

His words underscored the significance of The Waldorf-Astoria as a monument of hope for the future. They also connoted the realities of the Depression that gripped the country and the dire need for a symbol to alleviate the spirit of despair.

The Waldorf opening certainly hyped the city. For weeks afterwards, the streets and living rooms were abuzz with reports of the palatial splendors of the new hotel and the marvels of its construction: It was built on steel stilts and cushioned pads to counteract vibrations from the trains rushing to and fro in the tunnels underneath. It had its own railroad siding for well-heeled guests who pulled up in private Pullmans. And an illuminated driveway bisected the building between 49th and 50th Streets, enabling those who arrived by automobile to debark under cover and transfer themselves and their luggage to elevators east and west.

This driveway through the street-level center of the hotel was sheer genius from a security concept. Once a convoy escorted a VIP limousine into the driveway, it could be completely sealed off from East 49th to East 50th Street.

Elsewhere in the city, Norma Shearer and Clark Gable starred in "A Free Soul" at the Capital; "Grand Hotel" was playing live on the National stage; "George White's Scandals" of 1931 featured Rudy Vallee and Ray Bolger; two teenagers named Ginger Rogers and Ethel Merman had just become stars in the Gershwin musical "Girl Crazy"; and Eddie

Frank Farrell, retired "New York—Day by Day" columnist and author of this book, with old friend Ray Bolger, celebrated dancer and Broadway and film musical comedy star.

Cantor was heard on WEAF radio at 8 p.m. Sundays.

If Prohibition irked the sensible citizenry, it was surely hell on hotel revenues. There was no bar or cocktail lounge in the new Waldorf—a situation that required hasty alterations on Repeal. But, for the ingenious, there were devious ways to skirt the issue. I, for one, was familiar with an agent in the lobby who owned a van stocked with the best brands of alcoholic relief. His driver parked the van close to the hotel. And, for a set fee, the agent would deliver to your room a brown bag of "sandwiches" from the local deli. (He retired when sanity was restored to this land and opened a number of midtown restaurants.)

For the most part, guests resorted to pocket flasks. Discreet waiters brought glasses with ice to the tables.

Withal, there was a critical lull in legitimate business in that period. And The Waldorf was not immune.

George Boomer, son of Lucius, clearly remembers what hotel life was like in those dry, dismal Depression years. He was nine when the family moved from 300 Park Avenue to a Towers suite across the street. Their co-op apartment, for which they were offered $250,000 by Flo Ziegfeld in early 1929, wasn't worth a penny in 1931. They couldn't give it away. Lucius Boomer ultimately paid a man $30,000 to take the co-op off his hands.

Young George would rush home each day from Browning School to play baseball with the Waldorf employees. With 2000 on the staff and less than 300 guests in the 1852-room house, there were plenty of teams with time for baseball.

"And with 2000 employees," George sighs, "I was constantly under surveillance. Couldn't get away with a thing. . ."

He also recalls his father's anguish at having to slash the payroll by five hundred employees when the red ink warned danger to a crew of auditors.

Another indication of the grim situation

was that chambermaids were instructed to switch on lamps at twilight in unoccupied rooms and let them glow until midnight. The custom gave the hotel a lived-in look to the outside world and lessened the eeriness of emptiness for those within.

However, The Waldorf, like down-at-the heels royalty, never lost its touch of class. It always radiated an atmosphere of stateliness and savoir-vivre.

As described by a chronicler from The Times: "While the management was beating its brains out in the back offices trying to hold the financial structure together, the assistant managers on the lobby floor dressed and behaved like grand dukes. The uniforms of the bellhops, elevator operators and pages were always immaculate and expensive, and widely copied by other hotels. Each shift of uniformed employees came on duty in formation, marching into the lobby like parading Grenadier Guards."

And, while the cash drawer was almost empty, the larders were full—of pheasant, quail, guinea hen, squash, choice cuts of beef and lamb, venison, terrapin, lobsters and hedgehog. And guests ate off white china trimmed with gold leaf.

The Waldorf management reasoned that the Depression would not last forever. And their prestige would. They would simply wait out the hard times with optimism, laden with luxuries like fresh cut flowers adorning the lobby and redolent roses in silver vases on room service trays.

During the Depression, most of the city's hotels were taken over by banks or sold to new owners at a fraction of their real cost. The Waldorf's survival was attributed to several factors: outstanding executive management, remarkable esprit de corps on the part of the staff, the landlord's willingness to postpone the rent—and the intangibles of sentiment and emotion.

"The Waldorf always meant a great deal to a great many people," one authority noted. "It couldn't go under."

With Repeal, in March of 1933, the Men's Bar—a carryover tradition from the old Waldorf—opened its sanctified quarters to a rush of male "regulars." Now coeducational, the popular saloon continues to serves oversized drinks to both men and women under the sign of The Bull and Bear. And the "regulars" all have their own glasses with their initials etched thereon (compliments of the house) and stored visibly behind glass on the Bull and Bear wall ever ready for use.

Repeal also brought to the fore a knotty problem unanticipated in the original blueprint. Where to put a wine cellar? Fine wine cannot be disturbed by railroad rumblings. (And the hotel on stilts did not even have a full basement.) So, to avoid any reverberations, a wine "cellar" was hastily installed on the fifth floor, with proper temperature and climate. Repeal brought back the wines. Booze of every label was available. Champagne corks popped festively.

But the hotel remained in the red despite the boom of World War Two. There were long lines in the lobby begging for rooms and hordes of people pleading for tables in the various restaurants during the war. But there were also frozen prices and strict rationing which negated justifiable profits for the packed hotel.

At best, The Waldorf occasionally balanced the budget. Generally, the ledger still spurted crimson—until the controlling hand of Conrad Hilton grasped the managerial reins in 1949.

A Dream Captured

WHENEVER I THINK of the late Conrad Hilton and his acquisition of The Waldorf-Astoria, I recall a giant of a man, a formidable executive who had a fantastic dream which he determined would be his ultimate goal in life.

I also recall a friendly fellow who enjoyed every moment of the career he carved out for himself—a compulsive expansionist who actually achieved all of his loftiest ambitions during his own span of life.

And I recall a picture he kept for decades under the glass top of his desk—a picture of The Waldorf-Astoria on which he had penned with India ink: "The Greatest of Them All." For that was Connie's lifetime dream.

One can only imagine the frustration of author Thomas Ewing Dabney who in the late 1940s was in the process of writing a book about Conrad Hilton to be titled *The Man Who Bought the Plaza.* And, just when Dabney thought his book was finished and he was preparing for a vacation, he had to make a frantic return to his typewriter. It was 1949 and Dabney had to change his text and title to *The Man Who Bought the Waldorf*.

And how the plight of the publishers (Duell, Sloan and Pearce) who had to stop the action in the bindery and destroy all their suddenly obsolete titled and illustrated dust jackets?

Conrad Hilton's first tangible financial interest in The Waldorf was a large purchase of the hotel's debentures in 1942 when they were bargain-priced at $4.50.

Subsequently, Connie and a friend, Chicago financier Colonel Henry Crown, used their personal funds to accumulate common stock shares in The Waldorf-Astoria Corporation.

At that time, the board of Hilton Hotels did not have the slightest interest in acquiring The Waldorf because of its poor financial history. In 1949, The Waldorf-Astoria Corporation was in the red for $21,301,000. And at that time there were indications that the landlord (The New York Central Railroad) was considering the value of turning over management of The Waldorf to a major hotel system for more skilled, efficient and economic operation.

In these respects, the Hilton organization was a front-runner, especially due to its enviable guest referral advantages. However, the fussy railroad landlord had some ultra-conservative notions as to who should be given control of the treasured Park Avenue palace.

That's when Connie Hilton accumulated more common stock and started praying a lot.

Every morning at five, Connie would phone his public relations chief, Fred Joyce, who was a Catholic, and roust him out of the sack to attend first mass with him in St. Patrick's Cathedral.

Thereafter, each morning they would stroll around The Waldorf and gaze up longingly at the prize. Then they would have breakfast and go to work. My friend Joyce told me this prayerful procedure continued for weeks.

Conrad N. Hilton, founding father of the Hilton system, once told author Frank Farrell that he was a "compulsive expansionist." Above, Hilton displays the checks with which he took over the Statler hotels; the topmost was for $56,584,150. He continued expanding until, in some remote corners of the world, the name "Hilton" was thought to be the word for hotel in English.

There was something else on the plus side for Connie as far as the landlord was concerned. The fine quality of the Hilton management of The Plaza Hotel convinced the landlord that Connie respected a great property and knew how to preserve the decorum and traditions of a grand hotel.

Finally, on October 12, 1949, when Connie controlled 68% of The Waldorf's common stock with an investment in the neighborhood of $3,000,000, he gained management control of The Waldorf-Astoria.

Fred Joyce was first among those to breathe a sign of relief now that the pressure was off. At last, he was going to get a full night's sleep and return to a normal working schedule. Wrong. To his despairing surprise, his phone jingled at five next morning. It was Connie, waking him for first mass. What for? To offer thanksgiving.

Under the shrewd genius of Conrad Hilton, the books of The Waldorf began showing black within a year. The arrears in rent ultimately were reduced to zero by 1975.

The landlord began to maneuver to back away from the deal with Hilton. No way. Connie had a good lease. More than that, Connie owned the name Waldorf-Astoria.

Connie had not only proved the potential of the hotel to the landlord, but also to his own board of directors. Then he turned over the stock of The Waldorf-Astoria Corporation to Hilton Hotels Corporation at his original acquisition cost.

Bus traffic, mammoth truck freight haulage, air passenger traffic and air freight took their toll on railroads all over the nation. Railroads merged, wallowed, went out of business. The bankruptcy of landlord Penn-Central precipitated action re The Waldorf.

The acumen of Barron Hilton on the subject of real estate prompted his aggressive procedures to purchase the building and the ground under The Waldorf-Astoria. Sagaciously and with uncanny foresight, Barron closed the deal on April 26, 1977, for $36,000,000.

President Lyndon B. Johnson was host to Pope Paul VI in The Waldorf Towers' Presidential Suite. FACING PAGE: The Waldorf is also the New York home for both U.S. astronauts and Russian cosmonauts. Here, U.S. Astronaut Gordon Cooper is being decorated by then Mayor Robert F. Wagner, with Mrs. Cooper and the late Presidents Harry S Truman and Herbert C. Hoover adding their congratulations during a Waldorf reception. And longtime Waldorf residents the Duke and Duchess of Windsor are seen at a ball there. (PHOTOS: WILL WEISSBERG).

Under Barron's dynamic leadership, dividends have been increased seven times in the last six years. In fact, the dividend rate has more than quadrupled in that brief time span. And Hilton Hotels Corporation has expanded and diversified its role as an outstandingly successful manager of assets in the lodging and gaming industries. In Las Vegas, the Flamingo and the Hilton have become invaluable jewels in the Hilton treasury.

Unwilling to change The Waldorf radically in any way, except to upgrade it continually and care for it as a paragon in the eyes of the world, Barron Hilton—a tribute to his personal modesty and everlasting respect—resisted all suggestions to rename the hotel The Waldorf-Hilton or anything else. "The Greatest of Them All" remains today The Waldorf-Astoria.

What hath God wrought?

And what had Hilton bought?

Well, for sure, he had bought and paid for his father's dream.

He bought a hotel that General Motors saluted in advertising as the "Citadel of the gracious art of modern living."

Author Oliver Herford, on the occasion of the hotel's world premiere, wrote: "The Waldorf-Astoria brought exclusiveness to the masses."

Yet he bought a hotel so aloof that its sidewalks don't even touch the building. It is insulated against traffic vibrations by a ring of lead and asbestos.

A place that was editorialized on its golden anniversary in The New York Daily News as: "The hotel, in fact, has become a symbol of all that is grand about New York. We just hope the city will endure through good times and bad with the same style as The Waldorf-Astoria."

A hotel that's in the center of New York City's uptown financial district and office skyscrapers, surrounded by and within walking distance of almost every kind of temple of worship and a wide variety of department stores, restaurants and specialty shops.

A hotel in which a Protestant President of the United States, Lyndon B. Johnson, entertained the Vatican's Pope Paul VI, and also greeted and played host to a former Republican President, Herbert Hoover.

A hotel in which different members of the staff speak a total of 61 languages and where secretarial service is available in four.

A hotel that is always in step with period styles, the latest in modern illumination and fashion.

Wherein, on one day (May 23, 1963), the following events took place: There was an afternoon reception for 2,000 in the grand ballroom honoring Gordon Cooper and five other astronauts. The Duke and Duchess of Windsor returned home. Former President Hoover received the annual Circumnavigator's Club award. President John F. Kennedy paid a congratulatory visit to former President Hoover. Vice President Johnson moved into The Towers. General MacArthur was in residence. Former President Dwight D. Eisenhower was guest of honor at the American Iron and Steel Institute dinner in the grand ballroom that evening. Downstairs, at the same time, President Kennedy was

being honored at receptions in the Empire Room and Hilton Room. Former Vice President Richard M. Nixon was in residence. So was General Mark Clark, who was to be honored at a Father's Day luncheon.

A hotel in which one of America's most popular orchestra leaders, Peter Duchin, is musical director.

Wherein The Junior Leagues of America leased a handsome space in 1931 when the hotel opened and has been an important tenant ever since. In 1981, The Junior Leagues contracted for 38 rooms and two suites on an annual basis. Ergo, if the hotel were packed, but you had a friend in The Junior Leagues, you might still have been able to wangle a room in The Waldorf.

Wherein the kitchens served up a record 6,000 meals at noon one Sunday for an oversubscribed New York Police Department Holy Name Society communion breakfast.

Wherein star comic Danny Kaye did two benefit performances in one evening. I had invited him to do his thing for a charity in the main ballroom. Somehow Danny was intercepted earlier at the Park Avenue entrance and led astray into another charity party where he entertained for a half hour. When I phoned a Fifth Avenue apartment in which he was visiting and asked if he were ill, he told

New York's mayors are constantly seen at The Waldorf, as are a wide variety of internationally-known celebrities. Here, Danny Kaye with Clare Booth Luce (PHOTO: WILL WEISSBERG); then Mayor Robert F. Wagner greeting the late Indian Prime Minister Jawaharlal Nehru with former New York governor and U.S. Ambassador Averell Harriman; and former Mayor John V. Lindsay.

me he had shown up in The Waldorf earlier, performed and departed. I laughed and advised that he had been led to the wrong party. He moaned but got back into his tuxedo, returned to The Waldorf and was a smash hit, telling his audience about that evening's mistake—and a lot of other hilarious mistakes. That can happen in an inn with 28 reception rooms.

Former New York City Mayor Bob Wagner once declared: "During my terms of office, I think I spent more time greeting incoming VIPs at the entrance to The Waldorf Towers and at dinners in the ballroom than I spent at home." Waldorf employees called him "an unofficial member of the staff." Mayor John V. Lindsay became known affectionately as "Big John." And for "Little Abe" Beame, Waldorf carpenters created a platform called the "Beame Booster" to bring the mayor up to mike level behind the lectern.

A hotel which has played host to all the U.S. astronauts—and those Soviet cosmonauts who have visited New York.

A hotel which cleared a floor for and welcomed home all the hostages from the United States Embassy in Iran who had been held captive in Tehran under threat of death for 444 days. And discovered that the greatest thrill in the new-found freedom of the hos-

One of the assignments former Mayor Abraham D. Beame enjoyed was welcoming Britain's Princess Margaret to town.

Another great welcome at The Waldorf was upon the return of the hostages from Iran in 1981; they and their families were guests of The Waldorf and here hostage Barry Rosen is shown being greeted by Towers resident Mrs. Douglas MacArthur, widow of the legendary five-star general.

And Mayor Edward I. Koch had the pleasant assignment of presenting a New York City scroll honoring The Waldorf on its golden anniversary to Waldorf senior executive Frank Wangeman.

tages was being greeted at The Waldorf entrance by the widow of General Douglas MacArthur and Mayor Ed Koch.

A safe haven wherein one well-heeled, acutely hypochondriacal guest indulged his fear of bacteria to the extent that he reserved rooms above and below and all around him to avoid contamination from others.

A hotel which caters to both major debutante balls annually, the Yuletide Debutante Cotillion, sponsored by New York Infirmary, and Beatrice Joyce's International Debutante Ball. And little girls like Anne Rockefeller, Joan Kennedy, Dina Merrill, Brenda Frazier, Jackie Onassis, Lee Radzewill, Sandra Payson and others grow up and later return as sponsors and chairladies of charity balls.

And still it is not so highfalutin that it doesn't have "accommodations" for four types of "guests." There are those who pay The Towers rates and those who pay the regular room charges. Then there are the "statutory tenants," who moved in with yearly leases in the Depression years of the 1930s and who are still there at from $10 to $14 per diem—nine of 'em. And there are some Waldorf "guests" who pay nothing. They arrive nightly along the railroad tracks in cold weather and nest alongside the super-hot steam pipes which service the hotel above.

A hotel in which that late multimillion heiress Barbara Hutton tossed a "Plantation Party" which cost $200,000. It had live turf on the floor, live cotton plants and flowers and live horses in a corral. But when the procession of waiters arrived in marching order with the flaming desserts, they counted cadence to the same old tune, "Marching Along Together."

Where a giant bowling and billiards firm once leased "social-climbing" space in an effort to uplift its image from pool rooms and the classic observation that "a good billiard player is the sure sign of a misspent youth." Brunswick installed a tony Carom Club in The Waldorf as a courtesy to hotel guests and other VIP invitees.

A hotel located in the midst of a flock of other distinguished inns—the Ambassador, the original Park Lane, the Ritz-Carlton, the Chatham, Sherry's, the Marguery, the Madison, the Biltmore and others, all fine hostelries—that faded and died while The Waldorf was to survive and thrive youthfully.

Unforeseeably, Conrad Hilton's acquisition of The Waldorf spawned a veritable "university" for hotel execs. To be a "graduate" of The Waldorf-Astoria's distinguished list of staff executives is tantamount to a guarantee of an important job almost anywhere in the business.

European hoteliers have always scoffed at the idea that America could ever produce any illustrious innkeepers. Well, The Waldorf has forevermore corrected the impression that American hotelmen would always be desk clerks with "imported" superiors.

I was honored to be invited to the annual roundup of Waldorf alumni and alumnae in November of 1981. It was one of the most distinguished reunions ever. Former Waldorf execs from around the world assembled in the Hilton Room for cocktails and in the Empire

Many former debutantes eventually become chairladies of some of the many annual balls at The Waldorf. Among them is the lovely Dina Merrill, photographed with her actor-husband Cliff Robertson.

Room for an elaborate dinner, with cordials later in Peacock Alley.

Frank Wangeman and Gene Scanlan hosted. Guest and only speaker was honorary member General Carlos Romulo, who led off with three guffaw-worthy jokes and set the merry mood for the evening.

Anthony M. Rey, a former Waldorf Towers manager, served as toastmaster. He is the gentleman who pioneered the creation of the casino gambling hotel era in Atlantic City as president and chief exec of the first.

As Tony Rey proceeded to introduce celebrated guests present, it soon became obvious that the United States was no longer importing top level hotel execs. The Waldorf-Astoria is graduating and exporting them. The tide has turned.

Robert Huyot had flown in from Paris. This former Waldorf Towers manager had ascended to the presidency of the Intercontinental chain.

Former Waldorf men Walter Schnyder and Bodo Von Alvensleben had airlined in from Switzerland where Bodo is now director of the Hotel Beau Rivage and Schnyder is a hotel consultant.

Olive Barnett was on deck for honors. This former Waldorf exec is now one of Europe's most outstanding distaff hotel execs, managing things in London's fabled Savoy.

From Germany came Karl-Heinz Zimmermann, now owner and manager of the Hotel Weisses Rossle in the Black Forest.

And Alfred Krebs, who is owner-manager of the Grand Hotel Regina in Grindelwald, Switzerland.

Nicholas E. Behard jetted in from London where he is general manager of the Sheraton Park Tower.

However, this exportation of skilled innkeepers from The Waldorf to faraway places is not limited to Europe.

Ichiro Inumaru journeyed all the way from Japan to attend The Waldorf roundup as vice-chairman of the event. He is now executive veep and managing director of Tokyo's fabled earthquake-proof Hotel Imperial, which was blueprinted by the late American architect Frank Lloyd Wright.

Dieter Huckestein jetted from Israel where he is now general manager of the Tel Aviv Hilton.

Alex Braune, veep of Mexico's Posadas de Mexico and boss of the capital's Holiday Inn, junketed in from below the Rio Grande.

And from the island of Aruba came Milton Flueckiger, managing director of the Sheraton Hotel and Casino on that Carib paradise.

From distinguished domestic assignments were: Truman Wright, former assistant to Lucius Boomer and guiding genius behind White Sulphur Springs. . .

Arthur Surin, general manager of The Fontainebleau on Miami Beach. . .

Two San Franciscan celebs: Ernest Furstner and Bill Wilkinson. Furstner is now veep of Nob Hill's Fairmont. And Wilkinson is veep and general manager of Nob Hill's Stanford Court. . .

Gerald Sill, president and chief operating officer of Houston-International Hotels. . .

Henry Goldstein, general manager of Atlanta's Radisson. . .

John Kirk, general manager of The Adolphus in Dallas. . .

And Larry Kirk, general manager of the Denver Hilton.

Of course, there are countless other "grads" of The Waldorf who are now senior officers in blue ribbon hotels all over the globe, not mentioned here. I have had to limit myself to those I could identify at the November reception.

This seemed to me an ideal occasion for a memory test. So I asked everyone I chatted with if he could recall the motto of The Waldorf-Astoria? Each answered word for word, "The possible we do immediately; the impossible takes just a little more time."

And each explained to me that it was impossible for them to forget The Waldorf motto, because they have it in the back of their minds daily in the performance of their duties, wherever they are.

Stars of stage, screen, opera, the concert hall and even the prize ring are frequently seen at The Waldorf. Shown here are Douglas Fairbanks, Jr., Johnny Carson and Burt Reynolds at an annual dinner of a great entertainment world institution, The Friars; and singers Luciano Pavarotti and Leontyne Price at a ceremony at which they received awards for furthering goodwill between the United States and Italy (PHOTO: BOB SERATING).

*Two great personalities of stage and screen, Anthony
Newley and Barbra Streisand; fabled world
heavyweight champion Jack Dempsey going along
with the gag for singer Tony Martin and actress Cyd
Charisse; and motion picture star Alice Faye.*

Executive Suite

THE WALDORF-ASTORIA IS a $100 million a year operation. And the statistics on its maintenance and performance—staff, supplies and services—are staggering to compound.

Numbers are impressive. But the true sum and substance of the Waldorf can be measured better in terms of people.

When I comtemplate the enduring image of this grand and glorious hotel, it is mostly in the reflection of those who occupy the executive suite. For it is here, at the top, that the tone is set and the policy formulated to orchestrate the traditions of yesterday with the conveniences of tomorrow.

It is no easy task. It requires men of vision as well as operational skills.

And as I tabulate the composition of the command post, four names keep flashing through my mind: Conrad Nicholson Hilton, Barron Hilton, Frank George Wangeman, and Eugene Richard Scanlan. They may or may not be familiar to the reader, but these men are responsible for all that The Waldorf-Astoria stands for today. And each is a vital contributor to the legendary distinction of this golden inn.

The cast of characters in the hierarchy of The Waldorf-Astoria we celebrate today begins, naturally, with Conrad Hilton.

Conrad Hilton (known as "Connie" to friends and associates) checked out of this world at the age of 91 in January, 1979. He was a commanding figure, physically and psychologically, with enormous energy and irresistible charm. And he moulded an empire equally vast and impressive. He was big in stature, foresight and business acumen. He was also tenacious in his respect for truth and God and his country.

The man whose name became synonymous with the word "hotel" (indeed, in many lands, "Hilton" is thought to be the English translation for "hotel") was born, auspiciously, on Christmas Day, 1887, in San Antonio, then part of New Mexico Territory. His mother was of German descent.

His father, a Norwegian emigrant, had a mercantile business in the bustling little town. But the family income was augmented by the renting of rooms, primarily to traveling salesmen. And Connie's initiation into hoteldom began, in a sense, from his boyhood role of meeting trains to bring guests to the family abode, where rates were one dollar a day, including meals.

It was to be another two decades before he seriously entertained the prospects and profits of innkeeping. Meanwhile, he took odd jobs while attending school. After graduation from St. Michael's College in Santa Fe, he enrolled in the New Mexico Military Institute, then served as a lieutenant in the United States Army in World War One.

In the bleak postwar period, Connie paused to take stock of his life savings—all of $5000—and decided to buy a bank in the booming oil town of Cisco, Texas. When he got there, however, he had a change of mind.

The bank had upped its price. So he bought a hotel instead, the 40-room Mobley.

How significant that the banks and prime businesses went broke in the recession of 1920 and the area's oil supply ran dry, while Hilton's inn prospered! Then he proceeded to buy and build a slew of other hotels in his newly adopted state of Texas.

Connie Hilton was already recognized as the man with a golden touch when we first met, in 1940, at a movie junket staged by Warner Brothers in Sante Fe—the setting for an Errol Flynn-Olivia de Havilland film epic.

Among the stars and starlets who provided Hollywood glitter at the premiere was Rita Hayworth. As Connie and I ogled the auburn-tressed beauty, he recalled that Rita had started in show business as a Spanish dancer. And when the orchestra started playing "Put Your Little Foot," Hilton left our table and asked Miss Hayworth to dance. They gracefully glided into the Varsoviana, a dance I had never seen before. I was fascinated by their precision and grace (a la Astaire and Rogers), but I was also aware of the furtive movements of a strange man who kept following Hilton around the dance floor.

When the tempo changed to the more familiar (to me) foxtrot, I cut in on Connie and I advised him of the "following" he had attracted. Then I whirled away with the sultry screen star. Heady as I was with the radiant beauty in my arms, I also noted the man on the periphery was now following me.

"Do you know that guy?" I asked Rita.

She confided that he was her agent and boyfriend—and that he was insanely jealous! For years the character who shadowed our dancing was an inside joke between Connie and me.

Another recollection of that first meeting was that I, though many years younger, wilted at three o'clock in the morning and bade the party adieu; Connie, who had danced with nearly everyone there, was still going strong. Moreover, at eight a.m., when I yawningly shuffled into the dining room, there was Conrad Hilton, already finished with breakfast, regaling in a jolly reunion with a group of old friends.

This was the image I retained as I tallied his later exploits, his upward-and-onward climb to the pinnacles of success here and abroad.

The man who had coolly weathered the Depression, and boldly broadened his holdings when all others were shriveling, was now expanding his empire from coast to coast. In 1942, he resourcefully acquired the luxurious Town House in Los Angeles and The Plaza in New York.

Both were gems in his golden ring of inns. But there was yet another that he coveted that would be the crown jewel of all he possessed. And it was spelled out across the face of a picture he kept for years under the glass top of his desk. Across the silhouette of The Waldorf-Astoria, he had penned: "The Greatest of Them All!" It expressed his lifelong ambition. It represented his ultimate goal.

In 1946, The Hilton Hotels Corporation was founded with Condrad Hilton as president. And three years later, for the sum of $3 million, the organization gained operating control of the hotel of his dreams.

The long lease that Conrad Hilton negotiated for control of The Waldorf would stretch far beyond his 91 years on this planet. It would also pave the way for the climax before he departed.

When Barron Hilton purchased The Waldorf-Astoria outright in 1977, his father was 89 years old. Connie had lived to realize the apex of his lifetime dream.

All of which gave credence to his often voiced conviction that "man, with God's help and personal dedication, is capable of anything he can dream."

You would think he could retire then, resting on his laurels. But Conrad Nicholson Hilton, a human rival of nuclear fission, continued to work in his office until a week before his death.

Those who met him will never forget him.

And millions more will know him for what he left behind—a standard of excellence in a legion of hotels bearing his banner, if not his name.

Barron Hilton, who reigns today as chairman of the board, as president and chief executive officer of the Hilton Hotels Corporation, traveled a many-branched highway to reach this pinnacle in his multifaceted life.

The idea of becoming a hotel executive was as far away as the moon when he was a youngster. He was a straight-thinking, determined young man, resolute that he would make his own way in life. And he had a blueprint for that when he came out of the U.S. Navy at the age of 19 at the end of World War Two.

First he had a heart-to-heart session with his father (originally described by my late friend Whitney Bolton): "I'd like to talk to you about my future," young Barron began.

"Fine," Conrad Hilton agreed. "I hoped you would. Tell me what you think."

"I'm in love with a beautiful girl," Barron confided. "We intend to marry. We also intend to have children. Children means a nurse. Inside of a year, or less than two years after I marry, I'm going to have to have $1,000 a month to meet my domestic expenses. I don't think the hotel business pays that kind of money."

"You are exactly right," Conrad Hilton agreed. "It doesn't. I wouldn't pay anybody $1,000 a month to learn this business and it takes longer to learn this business than it does to have a baby. Good luck to you. When you get your figuring closer to earth and you think you want to come in at the bottom and learn the whole thing, I'll be here."

So young Barron went off to prove himself. First he married the girl he described, Marilyn Hawley (truly one of the most beautiful women I've ever met). He invested his savings in a citrus juice business. It clicked.

Next, he put together the Air Finance Cor-

poration which leased aircraft to commercial airlines. The Flying Tigers and Pacific Southwest Airlines were two of his customers.

With this financial footing, he was able to siphon some funds into professional football which he enjoyed so much. In 1960, he formed the Chargers team in Los Angeles, moving the franchise to San Diego a year later. Hilton's San Diego Chargers won four Western Division championships and one American Football League championship in five years. And, as one of the AFL founders, Barron served as president of the League for one term.

Almost everything young Hilton touched seemed to light up like the proverbial rainbow with a pot of gold at the other end.

In 1966, at the age of 38, Barron was elected president and chief executive officer of the Hilton Hotels Corporation. He had arrived there on his own merits, on his own terms.

Although Barron Hilton may appear to be a

Barron Hilton, chairman of the board, president and chief executive officer of Hilton Hotels Corporation, shares a laugh with the archbishop of the Roman Catholic diocese of New York, Terence Cardinal Cooke, during The Waldorf-Astoria's golden anniversary party. Because the topmost candle on the huge 50th birthday cake could not be reached by ladder, a messenger had to be rushed to St. Patrick's, the cardinal's cathedral, to borrow its tallest candlelighter (PHOTO: MATTHEW MAURO).

calm, solid, at-ease executive, sitting behind his desk in The Waldorf-Astoria, leisurely puffing away on a cigar, you sense the inner energy and drive emerging from the figure in the elegantly tailored suit. I sat in an armchair facing him, watching the smoke spiraling to the ceiling, and felt as if a rocket were ready to blast off at Cape Canaveral.

The day before I caught up with him, Barron had flown in from California for The Waldorf's star-studded golden anniversary celebration. The following morning he would board a Concorde for a speedy flight to London on business.

Would this be his first supersonic flight? He shook his head. No, he said; he had already flown in the latest and most sophisticated jet fighter, the F-15, courtesy of a friend, an Air Force general.

Flying happens to be his favorite sport. His particular passion is soaring—like a bird in the skies, silent and motorless. He is a licensed glider pilot and he frequently takes off from his ranch on the Nevada-California border for celestial spins over the Sierras.

Barron is also an enthusiastic rod-and-reel fisherman. And a first class shot with various barrel gauges. He hunts doves all over the map in September, duck from Pacific blinds in October and quail in Texas before the season ends.

He also enjoys golf. And is a prize-winning photographer. These pastimes, however, are just that.

First and foremost, he is a family man. He and his devoted Marilyn have eight children and three grandchildren. Weekend gatherings are lively affairs.

Born in Dallas on October 23, 1927, Barron settled in Southern California in 1935 and absorbed the Californian zest for sports and sun-worshiping. He remains, in his fifties, a handsome, tanned, athletic specimen with irrepressible stamina and a honed appetite for competition in all endeavors.

It is obvious he enjoys gamesmanship,

whether it is in the sports spectrum or the challenge of directing a network of hotels stretching from New York to Hawaii.

Barron Hilton is head of one of the nation's largest real estate holdings. He is host to more than 4,000,000 guests annually. And employer to a labor force of more than 32,000.

It's a demanding, multidirectional post. But he takes it in stride, day by day. There is, in a sense, the exhilaration of being a successful executive. Even more, there is the residual satisfaction of pleasing both guests and stockholders, and still having precious time with his family and hobbies.

Does Barron derive as much pleasure from being boss of The Waldorf-Astoria as Conrad Hilton did?

Without question, one of Barron Hilton's most satisfying acquisitions was the purchase in 1977 of the lessor's interest in the flagship of the Hilton Hotels fleet, The Waldorf-Astoria. The expenditure of $35.8 million made The Waldorf a wholly-owned property of the corporation. In addition to all the prestige the hotel brings to the Hilton tradition of hospitality, The Waldorf has consistently been one of the most profitable of Hilton's properties.

Barron entrusted Greg Dillon with the colossal task of assisting him with the evaluation and purchase of The Waldorf-Astoria. Dillon is executive vice president in charge of the burgeoning Real Estate Division of Hilton Hotels Corporation, which includes Hilton's rapidly growing franchise operations. He is also a Hilton board member.

Another of Barron Hilton's most valued advisors, William H. Edwards, was among the distinguished members of the board of directors who encouraged the acquisition of The Waldorf and the purchase of its land.

Edwards is president of the Hilton Hotels division, a position he maintains with all the expertise only forty years with Hilton can bring. He began his storied career in the hospitality industry while still earning his bachelor's degree at the University of Michigan. After the war he joined the staff of the Statler in Detroit and, on the acquisition of the Statler chain by Hilton in 1954, he moved to Chicago where he served as assistant general sales manager in Hilton's corporate offices in Chicago. His career with Hilton continued to progress to the point where he was elected to the board of directors and its executive committee in 1971.

As a leader among his peers in the hotel industry, Bill has been a member of the boards of the American Hotel & Motel Association, National Restaurant Association and National Institute for the Foodservice Industry, and was recently named to the newly formed Travel Advisory Board of the United States Department of Commerce. He is currently chairman-elect of the Travel Industry Association of America.

A recipient of many prestigious awards and honors, Edwards holds one position which is near and dear to his heart, that of the vice president of the Intercontinental Region of the Knights of Malta.

Before her marriage to top Hilton executive William H. Edwards, she was Peggy Nolan, a nationally starred songbird. She sang the theme song for The Waldorf's birthday party, "New York— New York."

While in law school at the University of Pittsburgh, Bill was assistant manager of the William Penn hotel in Pittsburgh. That's where he first met Ruth Ann (Peggy) Nolan who was then the inn's singing star. Peggy Nolan had just moved from Manhattan where she was featured with Al Donahue and his orchestra in the world famous Rainbow Room at Rockefeller Center. Bill was later to marry Peggy and begin their family. Their two sons, William Jr. and Bradley, are also prominent members of the hotel industry.

And it was the lovely Peggy Nolan who graced The Waldorf's ballroom stage during the golden anniversary reception to sing the theme tune, "New York, New York."

Frank Wangeman is senior vice president and director of Hilton Hotels Corporation— and executive vice president and managing director of The Waldorf-Astoria. He has another list of titles which could add a chapter to this book but I have a deadline and limited space.

How Wangeman achieved this lofty position in the world of renowned hoteliers is a feat comparable to advancing from private to general in the United States Marine Corps (with which I am personally familiar). It is a scenario replete with packing, traveling, unpacking; work, marriage, kids; more packing, traveling, unpacking; new hotel, new country, new schools, new friends; then pack it all up again, et cetera. . .

In 1945, a year of special significance for him, Frank Wangeman was already a veteran of international experience in innkeeping. He was, in fact, born to it. His father was managing director of Germany's famed Frankfurter Hof when Frank made his squalling debut in this world.

After graduating from the Swiss hotel school in Lausanne, he trained in some of Europe's most illustrious hotels: The Lausanne Palace, The George V in Paris, and The Ritz and Hyde Park in London. His first job in New York was with Lucius Boomer in The Waldorf-Astoria three years after its Park Avenue premiere. At the ripe old age of 23, Wangeman was The Waldorf's assistant manager.

Nine years later, Frank left to join the Hilton organization. He was then 33 and Conrad Hilton's personal chief of staff, subsequently to become chief operating officer of The Plaza in New York. That's where he first met the beautiful Marie Moyle of Salt Lake City. The year was 1945 and he was still a bachelor.

Marie was visiting the Big Apple with her dad, who was then head of the American Petroleum Institute for the Rocky Mountain area. Their good friends, Floyd Odlum and Boyd Hatch, top execs of the mighty Atlas Corporation, had booked the Moyles into The Plaza and fortuitously arranged introductions to Frank Wangeman.

It may not have immediately occurred to Wangeman—but it did to me when I first met her—that Marie could easily have been crowned Miss America (I had judged enough Atlantic City pageants to arrive justly at that conclusion). What did occur to the ultra-conservative Wangeman was that, in deference to the introduction proffered by tycoons Odlum and Hatch, it might be prudent to ask Miss Moyle for a luncheon date.

Along with pulchritude, Marie is gifted with an impish sense of humor. When Wangeman telephoned his luncheon suggestion, Marie coyly asked if it would be all right if she brought a friend. Wangeman envisioned sharing a Plaza table with two gorgeous females and readily agreed. The picture clouded slightly, however, when Marie showed up with another gentleman from whom she had previously accepted a luncheon invitation.

It was a frosty autumn day.

A few months later, however, Wangeman coincidentally found himself aboard a California-bound train with Marie's father. In that leisurely mode of travel, the pair had plenty of time to get to know each other. At one point Mr. Moyle asked Frank if he had ever seen a Western ranch. The European-born hotelier was fascinated by the prospect and, impulsively, decided to detour for a pause in Utah.

When they arrived in Salt Lake City, Wangeman's instinct for making the right decision was reinforced when he spotted Marie behind the wheel of a station wagon waiting to drive her father to the family ranch.

After dinner that evening, Marie casually asked Frank if he knew how to ski. Making that inquiry of a native of the Alps is like asking a kid if he likes ice cream.

Wangeman never got over that skiing date. He continued on his journey to Los Angeles and tried to concentrate on his new responsibilities, but his heart and much of his mind were in Salt Lake City. He slaved patiently, waiting for an opportunity to take a holiday.

The ultra-conservative "permanent" bachelor was hooked. While he toiled in Los

Frank G. Wangeman, then executive vice president and managing director of The Waldorf, was briefed by the State Department to bow to the Japanese emperor. But, apparently, Emperor Hirohito was briefed in Tokyo before his American visit about the Western custom of shaking hands. As a result, Wangeman bowed—and the emperor held out his hand for a shake on arrival in The Waldorf Towers' lobby.

Angeles, daydreaming of the wonders of married life with Marie Moyle, she was a carefree popular beauty in Salt Lake, completely unaware of his problem. And he did have a problem—a big problem—an almost impossible difference of religion.

Wangeman was a run-of-the-mill Lutheran. Marie was the daughter of the senior counselor to the president of the Mormon church. Mr. Moyle, due to his exalted and austere position among the hierarchy of the Mormon church, had a right to expect that his daughter would choose for a husband a gentleman of the same religious upbringing. Wangeman had no rights whatever. The barrier would seem insurmountable to most men.

Impulsively, Frank reached for the phone and dialed Marie's Salt Lake City number, made a luncheon date for next day and asked her to wear a certain suit, his favorite. Everything happened so fast, they can scarcely recall details.

They flew to Las Vegas, got married, then flew to Hawaii for a honeymoon. The one thing Marie clearly recalls: all she had with her was a purse. Cosmetics, apparel, everything else had to be purchased on the fly.

Needless to note, when Marie's parents were informed of the elopement, they were something less than ecstatic. To put it mildly, her father was on the verge of gunning for the groom.

Strategically the newlyweds bided their time, touring the islands, and took the slowest way home, sailing across the Pacific on a Matson Liner. By the time they stepped ashore in California, the shock had been absorbed. Marie's family was on the pier to greet them.

There were many who thought Connie Hilton was a bit myopic in 1949 when he originated Hilton International Hotels and dispatched Frank Wangeman to San Juan, Puerto Rico. There Wangeman's assignment was to build and organize the first of the Hilton International Hotels—The Caribe Hilton.

It was a herculean assignment for Frank who was just getting used to the luxury of his blue ribbon post as boss of New York's elegant old Plaza. It was like getting beached on sun-scorched coral in a formal business suit, armed only with a shovel and a blueprint.

And it was at a time in Wangeman's career when he had his heart set on attending the advanced management program in the Graduate School of Business Administration at Harvard University. Harvard would have to wait until Wangeman made a success out of the San Juan venture.

But the time he spent in San Juan, he recalls with a sigh, was a far cry from life in a tropical paradise. Putting the Caribe Hilton project together was a backbreaker beyond imagination.

It was not just that he was building a hotel from scratch. In the Puerto Rico of 1949, it was difficult enough to find experienced construction workers. But he also had to hire locals and train them as doormen, bellmen, chambermaids, cooks, waiters, bakers, telephone operators and clerks.

How often he silently blessed his father for sending him to the University of Zaragosa for, at least he was able to communicate in Spanish. He was also grateful to the elder Wangeman for his fluency in French (from the

Sorbonne in Paris). German, of course, was his native tongue; and English his second language. Then, too, he holds a diploma from the Aspen Institute for Humanistic Studies in Colorado—which abetted his ability to get along with people. With this background, and his own intuitive powers, Wangeman was able to assemble and establish the Caribe Hilton. It rose from coral sands to become the flower of Puerto Rico.

In 1951, Conrad Hilton paid a formidable tribute to Wangeman's talent by saddling him with more responsibilities. The Wangemans and their brood returned to Manhattan and a suite in the Roosevelt Hotel. He managed both the Roosevelt and the New Yorker from an office in the latter.

Next the Wangemans were on their way to California where he served for five years in the upper echelons of the Hilton executive headquarters. For the first time in their married lives, the Wangeman family's home was not a hotel. Frank bought an interesting house in Beverly Hills, previously owned by Groucho Marx.

Then came a cataclysmic choice. Wangeman was offered a number of tempting options as to his future. Frank and Marie discussed all, then narrowed the choices down to two.

He could more easily escalate his career within the capitol of the Hilton administration. Or he could assume the envied position of executive vice president and general manager of The Waldorf-Astoria.

Marie hastened to point out that the first alternative would require constant traveling around the world and he would not have much time to get to know his five children, much less be a father to them.

That decided matters.

Meanwhile Frank Wangeman was surprised to find another feather in his cap. Despite the fact that he did not convert to his wife's religion, the Mormon church accorded him an extraordinary tribute. In recognition of his professional expertise, Wangeman was elected to the board of directors of the Hotel Utah.

In 1960 the couple and their five children packed again and moved to Park Avenue. All the youngsters have since made other living arrangements (both daughters are married now).

As Marie and I spoke one autumn afternoon, I could not resist asking her what it was like to be the wife of a hotel chief, with room service twenty-four hours a day; with chambermaids and housemen, window-washers and such—and nothing to do.

She sighed and led me into a kitchen, pointing: "Here is where the daily meals are prepared." Then, with a grin, she added: "You have known Frank Wangeman for nearly four decades. So you know all too well what a strict disciplinarian he is. The children were never allowed to use the passenger elevators. They had to use the freight elevator. And God help any employee of the hotel who did anything in the way of special treatment for the kids. He had issued stern orders on the subject to everyone!"

One recent May afternoon, the Wangemans tossed a party in their suburban hideaway on Quaker Hill near Pawling, New York. One of their guests was a neighbor, Lowell Thomas.

When, at the high point of the party, Marie wheeled in a large and brightly lighted wedding cake, Lowell wondered aloud why that particular confection was ordered for dessert.

Marie dimpled in reply. It was, she announced, their 35th wedding anniversary. And, because they had eloped, this was their first wedding cake.

Eugene Scanlan, vice president and general manager of The Waldorf-Astoria, was the first chef in history to become a top executive of a blue ribbon hotel.

Gene was seventeen "and scared to death" when he strode out of the small town of Nanuet, New York, into the vast kitchens of The Waldorf on October 1, 1942.

Eugene R. Scanlan, vice president and general manager of The Waldorf, thinks of former Israeli Prime Minister Gold Meir as "the most gracious guest the hotel ever had."

French was the only language spoken in the kitchen then. And the words most familiar to the Irish-American apprentice cook were: *Ici!* (Here!) and *Stupide!* uttered with ferocity by *chef de cuisine* Gabriel Lugot.

A prerequisite for his employment, he recalls, was that he did not smoke. Later, the stipulation was elaborated upon: "If you smoke, you destroy the sense of smell. It is important to smell what you cook as well as to taste it."

Mr. Scanlan still does not smoke. He also observes another cardinal rule of his kitchen apprenticeship: "No alcoholic beverages before dinnertime."

More notably, today Gene Scanlan can converse fluently with French diplomats, artistes and Gallic chefs. He particularly relishes telling of lunching one day with Parisian singing star Edith Piaf. The "little sparrow" chirped away cheerily, then sighed: "One day if I could speak English the way the chef speaks French, I would be very happy."

He was also able to conduct a lively dialogue with Maurice Chevalier when that celebrated entertainer came to The Waldorf for a singing engagement.

However, the peak of his linguistic achievement—after four intensive years of spinning Berlitz records on his turntable—came the day he first summoned the courage to speak French to master chef Lugot.

"He had asked me to do something, and I said, 'Oui, Monsieur. Toute de suite (right away).' . . .And he turned to me with a quizzical look. 'Parlez français maintenant, Monsieur Scanlan?' I answered, 'Oui, Monsieur.' And his whole attitude toward me was different."

Scanlan smiled and shrugged. "You know, he really didn't think I was going to make it. Just an Irish-American kid in a French kitchen."

Well, the "Irish-American kid," whose rheumatic heart in childhood restricted him from participation in sports and other strenuous activities, never realized that his substitute play with the pots and pans in his mother's kitchen would secure an exciting future. He was destined to make strides that even he dared not dream were possible.

If there were hands that helped him along the way, a very influential pair belonged to René Black. René Black, one of the most cultured and intellectual personalities in the inn-keeping profession, was an accomplished artist, a discerning musical scholar, and he also happened to be in charge of all cuisines in The Waldorf. As Oscar's heir apparent, his title was chief of restaurants. And who was his favorite chef? Gene Scanlan, who then ranked number three in the kitchen.

And so it came to pass that a fabulous hotel was taking shape in Miami Beach in 1954. Its name was The Fontainebleau, and it "stole" René Black and his Waldorf expertise to launch the beachfront hi-rise. And Black, in turn, "stole" Eugene Scanlan from The Waldorf kitchen, promoting him to executive chef of The Fontainebleau. However, before Scanlan could cook anything, he first had to design all the kitchens in the new hotel. Scanlan reigned supreme in The Fontainebleau's culinary quarters until 1961 when Frank Wangeman lured him back to The Waldorf-Astoria as top chef.

Five years later, in an analysis of the Waldorf's food and beverage department, it was decided that Scanlan, the chef, knew more about food and beverage operations than anyone else. So he doffed his white hat and apron for the first time and became a business suit executive. In rapid order, the director of food and beverages became a vice president of the hotel and its manager within three years.

His crowning moment came when Barron Hilton bought The Waldorf-Astoria from the Penn Central Railroad in 1977. It was Eugene Scanlan who signed and handed over the check—for $36,000,000!

"All those zeros," he laughs, recalling the highlight of his (and Hilton's) career.

When Scanlan was elevated to the office of general manager in 1981, his boss, Frank Wangeman, declared: "I have always looked on Gene Scanlan as a guardian of The Waldorf tradition and the personification of Waldorf spirit."

For the genial, warm-hearted, erudite Scanlan, it has been "a labor of love" all the way. And it is with touching grace and modesty that he glibly extols the virtues and milestones of the hotel and lightly dismisses his own contributions.

"This grand old gal still has the ambience and charm of fifty years ago," he declares. "But she also has all the comforts of a new hotel, and the space and special touches that new hotels don't offer."

As he speaks, he initials staff directives with a bright green marker and fastens memoranda with green plastic clips. "A touch of the Irish," he chuckles.

The executive suite is no plush-lined ivory tower for Eugene Scanlan. It's where decisions, small and large, are rendered; and emergencies, minor or major, are attended. And it's where piles of mail, delivered twice daily, are deposited. The mail is no burden for Scanlan. Rather, it's a reinforcement of the esteem and sentiment with which the hotel is regarded near and far.

"The mail," he nods, "is one of the joys of running an inn. We get a lot of it, and it's all answered as quickly as possible. The best is from a happy guest who writes to say: 'I had a wonderful time. I enjoyed. Everybody was so nice. . .' That happens a lot."

In his time, Gene has cooked for popes, catered to cardinals, and sat with kings, presidents and prime ministers. The walls of his office are lined with photos of the great and mighty shaking hands with or embracing a beaming Scanlan.

But occupying stellar positions are two framed documents dear to his heart. One is a certificate of culinary apprenticeship certifying that:

"Eugene R. Scanlan has from October 1, 1942, to April 1, 1945, followed a course of Practical Culinary Training in the kitchens of The Waldorf-Astoria consisting of progressive rotation work in each division of the kitchen department—SAUCE, FISH, SOUP, ENTREMET, VEGETABLE, ROAST, GRILL, GARDE MANGER, BUTCHER, PASTRY, BANQUET. We therefore confer upon him the title of ASSISTANT CULINARIAN, which he merits for his observance of the fundamental principles of the profession, his application, good standing and serious character.

"We wish for him a constantly enlarging experience in all of the varied branches of the Culinary Arts.

[signed] "F. Ready, President; Gabriel Lugot, Executive Chef."

The other is the back of a menu, matted in red, its hand-written message large and clear and preserved under glass: "Dear Mr. Scanlan: If you had charge of hospitality in 'Bethlehem Inn' twenty centuries ago, the whole history of the world might have been changed—so gracious is your kindness. Thanks. With assurance of prayer—God love you—Fulton J. Sheen."

Indeed, it is a long road the "broth-of-a-bhoy" has traveled from the tidy little kitchen in Nanuet to the awesome sanctums of pots and pans, ovens and grills of The Waldorf-Astoria, and thence to the upper regions of the executive suite.

For him, it's been a thrilling, fulfilling trail

all the way. And with typical sunny-side-up optimism, he predicts: "The best is yet to come." We Irish are prone to mystical whimsy, so I may indulge the tendency with this postscript: That every anniversary The Waldorf celebrates is marked by Scanlan, too. On October 1, 1931, The Waldorf-Astoria officially opened its doors to the public on its "new" premises. And, on October 1, 1942, Eugene Scanlan walked through them for the first time as a new employee.

Richard Hahn is manager of The Waldorf. This is his second tour of duty on Park Avenue. His first assignment was as resident manager from 1967 to 1970.

During his lifetime in the hotel field, Dick Hahn has shuttled around the globe like the United States Marines. He was sitting pretty in 1980 as general manager of two Hilton Hotels in Cincinnati, the Netherland and the Terrace. He was that city's number one hotelier. Then came the call to return to New York. He didn't have to, but there is something irresistible about being an executive of The Waldorf-Astoria in the world of innkeepers. Sacrificing his pinnacle of success in Ohio, Dick Hahn and his family started packing. He moved into his new office on March 1, 1981.

As manager of The Waldorf, Hahn is back-up man for Wangeman and Scanlan and, in the chain of command, he is head man of the house whenever they are absent. But that is only one of his responsibilities. As soon as he got seated behind his desk, a $30,000,000 contract was handed to him. Starting in the spring of 1981, Hahn became overlord of The Waldorf's new air-conditioning system, which will be a three-year project.

That's not all. A few months later, Hahn became bossman of another major and tightly timetabled project, the modernization of Oscar's Restaurant, the popular eatery on the Lexington Avenue ground level. As other Waldorf innovations turn up, Hahn may gain another title, project manager.

Numbers . . .

As ONE, WHO IS ACCUSTOMED to the local versions of Duffy's Tavern and Archie's Place, I certainly have had cause to wonder why the price of a highball in my neighborhood oasis is so much less than in Sir Harry's Bar, located in The Waldorf's main lobby to the left as you enter from the Park Avenue side.

I have personally studied this subject at great outlay of cash over the years. I thought I had achieved a mite of expertise and a lot of burst capillaries in the process, but I never really understood anything until I was privileged to peek behind the scenes in The Waldorf. It can now be explained in terms of rent per square foot, lighting, decor-design, furniture, carpeting, fine crystal ware, security, etc.

Or, in a word, mathematics.

Albert F. Absy, vice president and comptroller of The Waldorf-Astoria, is a man who has been checking and double-checking numbers at 301 Park Avenue for decades.

Long before computers, there was Absy with the figures.

He can inform you that the going rent for shops in The Waldorf lobby runs between $80 and $100 per square foot per month, and that Sir Henry's Bar is in the $100 area. Space for a local corner pub leases for much less, perhaps $5 to $10 per square foot.

Mr. Absy can prove that The Waldorf paid $4,500,000 for combined utilities (electric, gas, steam and water) in 1975. But the total for the same utilities in 1981 was doubled—$9,000,000.

Lighting in the local tavern probably was designed by the owner or his wife. Lighting in Sir Harry's Bar was designed by an internationally famed illumination engineer and its ambiance created by an equally famous interior decorator.

The annual bill for uniforms and their care alone adds up to $325,000 per year.

The Waldorf-Astoria payroll in 1981 spiraled upward to $24,000,000.

Barron Hilton is a man who believes in keeping abreast of progress and, if possible, keeping far ahead of progress. He is a firm believer in spending a buck to make a buck, if it will enhance The Waldorf's appeal to its guests and make the bottom line appreciated by its stockholders. The competence of management can be measured by competition and achievement.

Two years ago, with energy costs escalating out of sight, Waldorf management summoned efficiency experts to determine how to reduce bills for heating and air-conditioning.

It was decided that a change from "weather-leaking" glass to thermopanes was necessary in the window-frames. This has been done almost without notice by hotel guests. Now there will be no drafts or drapes ruined by gales and blizzards. The new thermopanes will reject most of the sun's heat during warm months and will also reject the chill blasts of wintertime, thereby reducing accordingly the bills for heating and cooling. These thermopanes will also assure the guests of a quieter atmosphere by toning down the sounds of all external traffic and other sources of noise.

This thermopaning of The Waldorf will be followed with the installation of an updated central heating and air-conditioning system which will cost $10,000,000 a year for the next three years or a total of $30,000,000.

There are 21 jewel-box Otis elevators visible to guests in the various lobbies of The Waldorf. Behind the scenes there are 14 other service cars. The annual bill? During the period from 1977 to 1981, The Waldorf paid a total of $4,250,000 to Otis Elevator Company for modernization and maintenance.

Look aloft. There are hundreds of beautiful chandeliers in The Waldorf. All of these have to be lowered to floor level for cleaning by hand four or five times a year.

The Waldorf used to send out its laundry list of matchless linens, but no more. So many beautiful tablecloths and napkins disappeared that in 1981 the hotel installed its own laundry for these envied souvenirs.

Mark S. Lucas, Director of Front Office Operations for The Waldorf, wears three hats. He's in charge of reservations, registration and the mail room. The Waldorf does not wait for the post office to deliver; it sends a truck to the post office. The Waldorf's mail room is a kind of General Post Office by itself. It processes and stamps thousands of outgoing items daily. And it sorts, forwards and returns to senders thousands of pieces of incoming traffic, operating seven days per week. This souped-up postal service cost the hotel $193,843 in 1981.

"Rehab" is a term familiar to every member of The Waldorf staff, because it's going on all the time, on all floors all year round. Rehabilitation means repairs, fresh paint, dry cleaning, new drapes, new carpets, new lamps, upholstery, new furniture, new decor, modernization. In 1981 "rehab" cost The Waldorf $25,000,000.

The names of Ellen Lehman McCluskey,

Melanie Kahane, Beverly Hafner, David Williams, Catherine Churchill, Roland Lee and Elizabeth Sheen are a quick glance at the list of world-renowned decorators called in annually by The Waldorf for rehabilitation and refurbishing. Would you believe that The Waldorf pays out an average of $14,000,000 per year for this type of R&R? The bill for 1981 totaled $15,000,000.

The 1981 telephone bill was $2,700,000.

Someone had a golden idea for The Waldorf's 50th anniversary—to gild the twin turrets atop the hotel. They are now green, the color of weathered copper. However, the prudent thrifty management team vetoed the idea as too expensive for a little-appreciated cosmetic facelift.

In mid-1981, when interior specialist Melanie Kahane was retained to give Empire Room a new look, word got around that The Waldorf might be returning to a concept of starry entertainment in a 1982 cabaret.

In the 1930s, the Empire Room was the most prestigeous cabaret in New York. It served as a showcase for star attractions from all over the world. Every big name in show biz aspired to prove his or her talent in the

At home in a Waldorf suite.

Waldorf Tower residents
Frank and Barbara Sinatra.

Empire Room. Because, to be featured in the Empire Room proved that a star had reached the apex of success and was guaranteed bountiful bookings elsewhere all over the map.

The Waldorf became the paragon of United States hotels when it came to welcoming Third World personalities at the portals of The Towers—or welcoming a dazzling parade of entertainers.

I think my journalistic buddy Jack O'Brian expressed it better than anyone else when he wrote in his widely syndicated daily column:

"The Waldorf always was exclusive, but never bigoted. It was the first rrrrreally-big luxury hotel in New York not only to welcome black patronage, but held out such stellar entertainment as the Count Basie Orchestra, Sarah Vaughan, Ella Fitzgerald, Mabel Mercer, Lionel Hampton, Diahann Carroll, Harry Belafonte, Dorothy Dandridge and Lena Horne."

Then came the splurges in Las Vegas and Miami Beach with winter season peaks. The tug-of-war for star solo talent skyrocketed salaries. Individual talent became so rich that mobsters moved in on stars and offered them "better management" for a piece of the action. New York hotels wisely withdrew from such action.

How in the world could an Empire Room, which seats 500, conceivably contract for the song-and-dance routines of Mitzi Gaynor at $50,000 per week? Get our your pocket calculator and give yourself a rough estimate of what the old "cover charge" per guest would have to be to afford the little lassie. Besides, public tastes have changed. The clientele who popularize more intimate gathering places prefer candlelight and piano music. These evenings The Waldorf has pianos galore with headlining artists playing and singing behind them. Fans of superstars Mitzi Gaynor, Frank Sinatra and others purchase tickets to Radio City Music Hall, Carnegie Hall, Westbury Music Fair and various theaters.

A Hotel within a Hotel

THERE IS NO ADDRESS on the marquee. But a canopied entrance on 50th Street, near the southeast corner of Park Avenue—with pennants flying and liveried doormen scrambling to greet visitors arriving in chauffeured limousines—is the gateway to the most exclusive domicile in the world.

This is the famed Towers, The Waldorf-Astoria's "hotel within a hotel." It is second only to Buckingham Palace in playing host to crowned and titled heads of state. But the difference is that The Towers is also the home of more VIPs than any other single building.

From the 28th to the 47th floors of the Waldorf are The Towers suites—with one to four bedrooms and baths, living rooms, dining rooms, pantries, kitchens and servant quarters, all lavishly decorated and furnished, and available by the day, the month, the year.

In its time, The Towers has housed the most important figures in history—kings and queens, princes and prime ministers, heads

of state and industry, film stars, sports champions, front page celebrities—the rich, the famous, the powerful.

And, in its time, history has been made in The Towers.

In 1946, representatives of the United States, Great Britain, France and Russia—the "Big Four" of the Allied victory—met in The Towers to apportion the spoils and sign the peace.

It was the first time a treaty council had been held on American soil since Russia and Japan met at Portsmouth, New Hampshire, to sign the Treaty of 1905.

The ministers had previously met in the satin and gilt luxury of the Palais du Luxembourg in Paris. Now they were to convene in New York. But neither the federal government, the state, nor the city had a proper place to shelter them. So the State Department asked The Waldorf-Astoria if it could provide space for a six-week meeting of the Council of Foreign Ministers. And, lo, it was done: 100 rooms for offices, 75 rooms for staff and 10 rooms for "principals."

Discommoded guests were soothed by the patriotic scope of the move. And the renowned Waldorf efficiency rose to its finest heights. Overnight, rooms stripped of bedroom furniture became offices. House telephones were removed and a 25-trunk switchboard was installed, manned by multilingual operators.

Washington sent a great oval table with 21 chairs, and the flags of the Big Four were arranged alphabetically against the wall of the 30' × 50' conference room.

Room service noted the drinking preferences of the ministers: cognac for the French; Scotch (with water, no ice) for the English; bourbon and branch water for the South Carolinian Secretary of State James Byrnes; and, for the USSR's Molotov, light wine and an occasional hooker of brandy, Scotch or bourbon. No demand for vodka.

When it was over, it was noted that the Waldorf hospitality had been instrumental in the Allies' initial achievement of postwar harmony. In Suite 37A of the Towers, terms for treaties dealing with Italy, Bulgaria, Hungary, Yugoslavia and Finland had been historically and amicably agreed upon.

Obviously The Waldorf served as birthplace for the United Nations.

The Waldorf adopted a policy of caring for every nation in the United Nations with the same courtesy and consideration, no matter what its size or influence.

Not for naught has it been said that if The Towers' walls could talk, oh, what tales could be told . . .

This was vividly brought home to me the morning I shared a breakfast hour with General Carlos Romulo in his Towers suite. The only living signer of the 1945 United Nations Charter had just passed his 82nd birthday. But the dynamic octogenarian had lost none of his incredible energy, nor his infallible memory for dates and details. And, in the intimate setting on this autumnal day, the esteemed Filipino patriarch confided a stirring sequence of now-it-can-be-told stories.

It was 1936 when young Carlos Romulo first arrived in Suite 3600, accompanied by President Manuel Quezon. The Philippine Commonwealth Government had just been established and Quezon was its first president. In this concrete step towards eventual independence, both the United States and the new Philippine government recognized the need

to strengthen the Islands' defenses against the threat of Japanese militarism.

A series of tactical meetings were held in Towers Suite 3600. And into the dilemma of how to raise an army, train an army, and who could command it stepped the bustling, bow-tied Roy W. Howard, head of the Scripps-Howard newspaper chain. My late boss and personal friend knew just the man for the job. His name was General Douglas MacArthur and Roy Howard would recommend and propel his appointment all the way through President Franklin Roosevelt.

The rest, of course, is history. And no one knows it better than General Romulo. He sighed as he recalled how he, MacArthur and Quezon were forced to withdraw from Manila when the Japanese invasion came, New Year's Eve, 1941. The triumvirate escaped briefly to the rocky fortress of Corregidor. "But," he grinned, "we had not lost our sense of humor. We wished each other a 'Jappy' New Year."

The years pass. Romulo, again ensconced in Suite 3600, learns from Senator Warren Austin that Philippine independence is officially recognized. The banner day is July 4, 1946.

Senator Austin becomes the first United States Ambassador to the United Nations, and again meets with Romulo in Suite 3600 to show him the original design for the United Nations flag. The General shakes his head. "No, that's not right. The Philippine Islands are not shown in this conception."

Austin explains that, in such a compressed design, the Philippines are too small to be located. General Romulo argues that Manila and the Islands could be represented by a dot in the UN symbol. He won his point. If you study that symbol, you will find Romulo's dot.

From the initial establishment of the United Nations in New York, it was decided that the United States ambassadorial residence would be in The Towers. Only The Waldorf Towers could provide the space, the proximity, the dignity and security requisite to a United States Embassy. And when the Greal Seal was affixed on the door of the 7-room suite on the 42nd floor of The Towers, it became the first and only ambassadorial residence in a hotel in the world. And the first to move in was Ambassador Henry Cabot Lodge.

General Romulo has been a guest of every United States Ambassador to the United Nations who has resided there. He was particularly close to Ambassador Adlai Stevenson. He made the elevator trip, six floors up, frequently—the first time to see how Stevenson had embellished the decor of the Embassy suite.

As soon as he moved in, Stevenson had ordered the pictures then there removed and replaced them with art works loaned him by the Museum of Modern Art. The ambassador was in an ebullient mood as he expounded on his love of modern art. On another occasion, however, a concerned Romulo was invited to the 42nd floor by a despondent Stevenson.

The emergency call was prompted by the Cuban Bay of Pigs incident. The ambassador confided to Romulo that the Kennedy administration had failed to communicate with him on this delicate maneuver. He was, he said, prepared to resign because he could not possibly parry the questions which would come at the UN the next day and he felt he—and his post—would lose face. Romulo solemnly reasoned with the agitated ambassador. And talked him out of the resignation.

Over the years, as longtime regular residents, the general and his wife shared friendly relations with many Towers neighbors of note. The closest, of course, with General Douglas MacArthur, whose widow, Jean, maintains the lodgings—and the sentimental ties. Romulo smiled as he told how he accompanied Mrs. MacArthur to a football game at West Point in the fall of '81 and they received a standing ovation!

Lowell Thomas, whose Manhattan address was always The Waldorf, was another intimate of Romulo. As fellow octogenarians,

The late Lowell Thomas, world traveler, writer and commentator.

they shared years of history—albeit in different directions.

Lowell, in a pique of mock exasperation, once collared Romulo: "People are forever asking me dumb questions: Why am I skiing at the age of 85? What do I eat? What do I do to have such get-up-and-go?" The world traveler and commentator shrugged and grinned. "I have finally doped out a stock reply: As I look back over the past, I cannot remember ever tasting yogurt or Geritol!"

Her Excellency Jeane Jordan Kirkpatrick, our United States Ambassador to the United Nations, now serves in The Towers. She has been called "Reagan's heroine," for the intellectual brillance she has brought to the UN as a hard-line neo-conservative.

Were you to ring the buzzer of another Towers suite, as I have done many times, you might expect John Kluge to answer. He's the financial genius who heads Metromedia, the conglomerate which provides an umbrella over multiple enterprises in the communications, entertainment and advertising worlds. New York TV's Channel 5 and radio's WNEW are two lively outlets in the Metromedia family in Manhattan, so don't be surprised if talk-show superstar Merv Griffin answers the doorbell. Whenever Merv is in the New York area, he is frequently Kluge's houseguest. Or you could be in for another surprise.

Mr. Kluge does not remotely resemble your typical athlete or gymnast, but he is a firm believer in keeping fit and occasionally he is called upon to prove it. Once I arrived for cocktails and found John standing on his head atop a barstool, no hands. He must have specially tailored pants. Nothing fell out of his pockets.

Mrs. William Woodward, matriarch of New York social life and the nation's most respected thoroughbred racing stable owner, was the "hostess with the mostest" in The Towers. Her spacious Suite 31-T will ever be remembered as the setting for the most glamorous private parties in the Big Apple. Elsie's invitations were "command performances." As I strolled home from her starry soirées, I was never able to recall the names of all the celebs I had rubbed elbows with in one evening. She died in 1981 at the age of 98.

If you reside in The Waldorf, it seems, you will live a long time. On that nonagenarian theme, I recall the stirring philosophy of General MacArthur. When a reception was planned in honor of his 80th birthday, the general asked me to put this motto on his cake: "Youth is not a time in life. Youth is a state of mind."

If youth is a state of mind, then Frank Kelly, bell captain of The Towers, is very young indeed. "Kelly," as he's known to one and all from President Roosevelt to President Reagan, was born August 10, 1903, and spent "the best 38 years of my life" in The Towers.

In that span, he has greeted and been embraced by the most famous personages of the century.

He was there when FDR arrived at The Waldorf's own railroad siding and made his way from his private Pullman car to a special Towers elevator without ever leaving hotel property.

Cars on the railroad siding are now used as storerooms for china. And the babies that Kelly "carried in my arms through the halls" are now grown, with children (and dynasties) of their own.

And, young or old, they always stop by Kelly's desk. "One of the Arab princes comes with his son now. And he always says: 'Kelly, tell my boy how long you know me.' "

Not long ago an ailing Duchess of Windsor returned to The Towers, which had been the ducal residence from the time Edward abdicated as King of England for "the woman I love. . ." As the Dutchess hobbled into the lobby, she paused and sighed. "Now I know I'm home," she smiled, "I see Kelly."

Kelly remembers meeting the Duke and Duchess at the North River pier, when sleek liners were the mode of travel, to transport their massive luggage across town to Suite 28A. He also recalls "the war years, when The Towers looked like a military compound with all the big generals, European and American, staying here. We even had Clark Gable in uniform."

Then there was Winston Churchill, in his zippered air-raid suit, looking something like a stuffed panda. "A grand old man," says Kelly." Always a cigar, always a smile, always something nice to say . . ."

He had a special fondness for former President Herbert Hoover, who made The Towers his home from the time he left office. "I always remembered his birthday, because it was mine, too. And I would say: 'Happy Birthday, Mr. Hoover—two great men were born on this day.' And he would laugh.

"Despite his cold, solemn appearance in public," Kelly recalls, "Mr. Hoover always liked to have children around. He always had a supply of doodads and souvenirs for youngsters who came to visit. My boss Frank Wangeman's kids frequently dropped in. Mr. Hoover once told me, 'Always remember that a child is the only one who will always tell you the truth.' "

Kelly remembers Cole Porter as "a little man in great pain; he walked with a cane (all those operations after his riding accident) and always wore a big Texan hat."

The Waldorf presented the composer with a Steinway grand piano. And room service delivered a pitcher of martinis daily at 10:30 a.m. The rings from booze glasses which provided, we presume, titillating inspiration, are still apparent on the rim of the beautiful beflowered grand which is now on view (and played nightly) in Peacock Alley.

And the Porter suite, which has costly flooring from a French chateau, in now occupied by another musical celebrity, Frank Sinatra, who spent $400,000 redecorating it to his wife's taste.

"Oh, yes, Sinatra is a permanent here

Crown Prince Akihito of Japan and Princess Michiko arrive at The Waldorf.

now," Kelly nods. "And I remember when you couldn't get into the lobby when he was singing in the Empire Room. And we had to be on guard, because all those bobby-soxers were trying to get past us to find a way to get near him."

A strict edict, dutifully obeyed, is: "Never, never ask for an autograph." Beyond that, it's a matter of instinctive good manners, courtesy and protocol. "We always say: 'Nice to have you with us, Mr. Ambassador,' and shake hands. Except with the Japanese. Then we bow. And they bow back. They're beautiful people, they have a style of their own."

Protocol is second nature to The Waldorf staff. And nobody knows it better than the top brass. So, when it was announced that the Emperor Hirohito would make his first visit to the United States on October 5, 1975, and check in at The Towers during his New York stay, everyone brushed up on the prescribed diplomatic etiquette for the occasion.

Frank Wangeman spent hours in his office reviewing courtesies and Japanese religion and customs. Paramount in his mind was that one must never touch the person of the Japanese Emperor. One must bow, not shake hands.

At the same time, across the Pacific, Emperor Hirohito must have been briefed on American customs and courtesies.

And so it happened that East and West collided at the entrance to The Towers. Wangeman bowed. And Emperor Hirohito extended his hand enthusiastically.

Furthermore, in an elevator packed with Japanese security and U.S. Secret Service agents, there was no way to avoid bodily contact with the Emperor.

At the door of the Presidential Suite, a flustered Wangeman bowed again. And again, the Emperor smiled and vigorously shook the hotel exec's hand.

Afterwards, Wangeman asked if there was anything he wished. The Emperor said, yes. He would like to invite Mrs. Douglas MacArthur to his suite—to pay his respects to the widow of the man he had learned to call "friend."

Protocol can be a routine affair. Or it can get ticklish—in a feverish, or humorous vein.

The late King Faisal of Saudi Arabia made The Waldorf his New York home.

Waldorf Towers greeters are accustomed to handling every type of surprise. When the aging King Ibn Saud, venerated ruler of Saudi Arabia, arrived on his last visit, one of his aides mentioned that the retinue included a herd of goats, because goat milk was a most important item on His Majesty's menu. Carpenters were summoned immediately to devise a pen in a corner parking space of the driveway.

Or the time when a Crown Prince decides to remain in New York for another week—and his suite has been reserved in advance by another chief of state.

One particularly edgy crisis erupted prior to the arrival of Queen Elizabeth and Prince Philip. Arrangements had been made for Britain's royal couple to stay in the Presidential Suite.

Saudi's Prince Faisal was occupying the suite that week. The situation was explained and an offer was made to move him to comparable quarters. Faisal, however, refused to budge. Management was nonplussed. What

The late President Dwight D. Eisenhower and his wife, Mamie, celebrated his election to the presidency of the U.S. at a Waldorf reception and were frequent visitors before and after.

to do? At a top-level meeting, it was noted that the Duke and Duchess of Windsor were sojourning in another part of the world; their suite was empty. Why not use it? So 28A was hurriedly transformed into the Royal Suite. (And Her Majesty never knew she was sleeping in her uncle's bed.)

Also, frantic juggling for nearby quarters was necessitated by the extensive entourage accompanying the Queen and her consort: Scotland Yard security, ladies-in-waiting, valets, pages, footmen, and the rest. Needless to say, it was done, and the 28th floor soon bristled with British accents and 4 p.m. calls for high tea.

Sometimes the diplomatic measures exercised by Towers employees exceed normal protocol. Behind the scenes, for instance, they diligently maneuvered to make sure that General MacArthur and President Truman (the commander-in-chief who relieved the general from his Korean War command) never boarded the same elevator.

Ditto MacArthur and Eisenhower. The relationship of these two West Pointers chilled in 1952 when they competed for the GOP presidential nomination.

Actually, Dwight Eisenhower did not occupy the formal Presidential Suite on the 35th floor. Mamie had "a high altitude problem"; so management set up an alternate Presidential Suite on the seventh floor, with access to The Towers elevators. They even furnished the new suite with Mamie's favorite antiques and colonial Williamsburg decor.

The alternate suite became the favored residence of another presidential couple, former President Gerald Ford and his wife, Betty; they preferred it because Mrs. Ford also suffered from a mild case of acrophobia.

The most severe form of the malady was exhibited by Bing Crosby. The seemingly devil-may-care songman was so leery of heights, he literally swooned from peering out a second-story window. In guarding his secret phobia, management created a Bing Crosby Suite, 567-69. In those rooms, Bing could verily jump out of the window without getting hurt. The roof of the ballroom was less than three feet below the sill, and it was covered with outdoor carpeting—so wherever the singer gazed, he perceived a comforting meadow of green.

Some VIPs request and get minimal fanfare. Winston Churchill, Prince Ranier and Princess Grace, Nikita Khrushchev and Charles de Gaulle were among the unobtrusive guests. The only distinction requisitioned for the French president was the longest bed in the house. Khrushchev brought along his own chef, only to spent his time in the kitchens, learning Waldorf recipes.

Robert Briscoe, the Lord Mayor of Dublin, insisted on no protocol and no bodyguards when he stayed at The Towers. He was a gregarious soul and enjoyed talking with people. So, one day, when he got into The Towers elevator, he cheerily greeted the two men in the rear of the car. By the time the lift reached the 28th floor, the Lord Mayor had invited William Dasheff and Ted Lynch, reps of the Reynolds Metals Company, to share a bit of Irish whiskey in his suite. The pair explained they were on their way to visit Richard S.

Reynolds, Jr., and David P. Reynolds, who were Briscoe's next-door neighbors. So, instead, the Lord Mayor accepted their invitations to the Reynolds' preserve for a spontaneous round of mirth and merriment.

If protocol snags at The Waldorf, it's rarely the fault of the accepted experts. More often it's a snarl of traffic or tangled airline schedules that can cause near-confrontations of alien personalities at The Towers doorstep.

On one specific occasion, Towers management avoided a Middle East collision by rerouting a motorcade. There was bedlam in the heavily patrolled lobby when a Secret Service agent stationed at LaGuardia Airport shortwaved that a plane from Washington with Israeli Prime Minister Menachem Begin aboard had arrived and the convoy was on its way to the hotel.

Meanwhile, the prince of an Arab nation had landed at Kennedy Airport, three hours earlier than expected. The man behind the desk at The Towers felt faint. But instead of reaching for smelling salts, he buttonholed a Secret Service agent. "Do something!" he pleaded.

Luckily, the agent was able to alert his counterpart at Kennedy by radio and recommend that the Kennedy contingent take the slow, "scenic route" to Manhattan. So the Arabian motorcade went the way of crafty cab drivers, all around the Belt Parkway.

Another Middle East crisis was, in a sense, precipitated by our State Department. Veep Eugene Scanlan cringes as he recalls the episode.

One of his favorite people, Israel's former Prime Minister Golda Meir was in the house when word came that the State Department was reserving a suite for a Very Important Person. "They gave us a fictitious name," Scanlan recalled, "until the day of the official arrival. Then we were told that the PLO's Yassir Arafat would be staying in The Towers. It was, they insisted, the only safe place to put him."

In the uproar that ensued, there were

Prime Minister Menachem Begin of Israel.

threats of bombs from protestors and cancellations from major Jewish organizations. But the critical situation was placated by the diplomacy of Mrs. Meir who consoled Scanlan: "I know you have an unwanted guest staying here and I know it isn't your fault. The Waldorf will still be my home in New York whenever I come here."

Scanlan thanked her for understanding and asked if he might quote her. Certainly, she said. And saved a lot of misunderstood grievance.

When Prime Minister Menachem Begin and his wife were in The Towers for the first time, Scanlan asked Mrs. Begin if he might be of assistance in any way. Mrs. Begin hesitated, then admitted there was something—if he could get her some Bazooka Bubble Gum for her bubble-blowing grandchildren home in Israel. How would it look for someone in her position loading up with bubble gum, which was unobtainable in Israel? Mrs. Begin and Scanlan laughed at the thought of it. That day and whenever she was visiting her suite was always stocked with bubble gum.

And it was so inscribed in the archives, in the same meticulously maintained register that listed Churchill's favorite brand of cigars, Hoover's choice of cheese, Hirohito's preference for American oatmeal for breakfast, King Peter's penchant for cheap candy, and jelly-beans for guess-who?

You don't have to be a president, a prime minister, a prince, or even a chief of state to reserve the Presidential Suite in The Waldorf Towers.Corporate executives (and other monied moguls) frequently check in at $1,900 a night.

Actually, any reputable guest with the wherewithal can enjoy the luxury of the high-ceilinged quarters with the many-windowed view. You can roam the rooms where statesmen dwelled and feel the impact of history. You can touch history, too, sitting in President Kennedy's rocking chair, or at General MacArthur's desk.

And Then
It Happened. . .

THERE ARE MOMENTS IN time indelibly etched in one's memory. Singular events such as graduation, marriage, the first-born child.

Then there are memories shared by millions—equally vivid. We can, all of us who were on this planet at the time, recall exactly where we were and what we were doing the day Pearl Harbor was attacked, the day President Kennedy was shot and the night the lights went out on the East Coast. . .

If anything, the big blackout of November 9, 1965, proved indubitably that The Waldorf-Astoria could handle a major crisis with calm and elegance.

When a wrench in the works near Niagara Falls caused New York City and the entire Northeastern United States—plus a large section of Canada—to be suddenly thrown into darkness, The Waldorf faced the event by bathing itself in the romance of candlelight supplied by the banquet department.

Candles gleamed on desks in the lobby and tables in the restaurants. And thousands flickered in the candelabras of the grand ballroom where the closing dinner of the National Commercial Finance Conference was being held. The entire reception, dinner as planned, musicians playing and the guest of honor speaking, rolled merrily, albeit dimly, along. The hushed atmostphere readily compensated for the lack of microphones.

All members of the staff conscientiously remained at their posts.

Where was one to go in a city shut down by lack of power, underground and vertical transportation? The Waldorf restaurants, for one. Peacock Alley, the Bull and Bear and Oscar's served guests throughout the evening. The ice held out until after midnight. And when clean dishes were hard to find, paper plates and cups were utilized—for the first time in the hotel's history.

In The Towers, those accustomed to special service were not disappointed. Caviar had been ordered for a cocktail party in progress on the 40th floor. And, when it was reported the ice had melted, a busboy was dispatched to climb the stairs and deliver another bucket.

Among those who decided to climb stairs to their Towers apartments were Mrs. Douglas MacArthur and Mrs. Carlos Romulo, who had been chatting in the lobby. Valiantly they got to the seventh floor and sent out an SOS. Management responded to their distress with candles and rooms for the night on the seventh.

As often happens, crisis had evolved into a form of revelry, a certain camaraderie. When it was over, The Waldorf issued membership cards to all who had been there. They were duly engraved:

"The Waldorf-Astoria Blackout Club—In recognition of participation and cooperation as a wonderful guest on the dark night of November 9, 1965, in New York City."

The card entitled the holder to "priority for seating in either the Bull and Bear or Peacock Alley on the night of the next blackout."

It seemed like a funny idea at the time. Certainly, a long shot. But a dozen years later, the lights went out again.

On July 13, 1977, The Waldorf was busy preparing a tricolor salute to Paris, the City of Light, in honor of Bastille Day, the fourteenth of July.

Conrad Hilton was in his suite on the 36th floor preparing for a flight to Switzerland.

The restaurants were still serving dinner; guests were still checking in.

And, at 9:31 p.m., the entire city was plunged into darkness.

Once again, The Waldorf rose to the occasion. This time, perhaps, with an extra ounce of preparedness.

And, once again, lower ranks of the staff voluntarily exceeded all measures of self-sacrifice and rose to such stature in trying to help in the emergency that it was positively heroic.

Some 5,000 candles were on hand, to be sand-anchored in styrofoam cups, given out at the registration desk and delivered to those stranded in upper-floor rooms.

The Hilton VIP limousine rolled into the driveway to cast its headlights into the lower lobby.

Coffee, doughnuts and fruit punch were ladled elegantly from tables set up in the lobby. And, as the night wore on, lounges, ottomans, pillows and blankets were spread for the weary.

Workers on their way home returned to serve in whatever capacity needed. Retirees who lived nearby also volunteered their services. Front office personnel assumed all manner of posts, from bellmen to switchboard to security patrols to candle-holding assistants to the chef.

A man in Suite 42C telephoned to say that he and his wife just arrived from Columbus, Ohio. "We are hungry and would like something to eat."

On the 35th floor Conrad Hilton was prepared to forget about the food order he had telephoned in earlier; then his buzzer

OVERLEAF: A major Waldorf banquet continues by candlelight despite the total New York blackout on the night of November 9, 1965.

This will confer upon

membership in

The Waldorf-Astoria

BLACKOUT CLUB

in recognition of participation
and cooperation as a wonderful guest
on the dark night of NOVEMBER 9, 1965
in New York City

Executive Vice-President
and General Manager

Vice-President
and Manager

sounded. He was startled to find his food on a tray in the hands of Conrad Wangeman, son of the Waldorf exec. Connie invited the youngster to sit and rest up after his mighty climb. Young Wangeman was grateful, but he couldn't pause. He still had another order for a guest seven floors higher.

At 8:30 p.m. the next evening, power was restored. An hour later, the wax-scarred carpet had been cleaned, debris cleared away, electric ovens were working and Peacock Alley, with a tired staff and limited menu, reopened for business.

As the welcome whirr of the elevators transported the last guest to the upper floors, there was nary a sign that anything had disrupted the normal proceedings during the past twenty-three hours.

Today the hotel has it own emergency generators insuring the operation of at least one elevator in each bank. And while it doesn't relish the notion, it is thoroughly prepared for any future electrical emergencies.

The blackouts of '65 and '77 affected millions of people in large geographic areas. But there was one blackout reserved for The Waldorf alone. And staffers recall it with a mixture of emotions. A grimace here, a chuckle there and, for all, a heady sigh.

It was the telephonic blackout of November 25, 1979.

Billed as "Dimension Feature Package 9" —a two million dollar computerized telephone system—it was installed in the wee hours of November 24th on an otherwise tranquil Saturday morning on the Thanksgiving weekend. Almost from the start Dimension 2000 (as it is called now) caused a giant headache.

For one thing, many of the room numbers had to be changed to conform with the system's new phone numbers. And some guests returning after a night out couldn't find their rooms at all.

In particular, there was the woman from

South Windsor, Connecticut, whose room number had been changed while she was below in the lobby. Describing what followed, she shuddered: "I thought I was having my breakdown. I went upstairs and my room had disappeared. I searched for a while and then I decided to go and get my husband in the lobby. But I said to myself, 'Wait a minute, you're 48 years old, you can read numbers and you can handle this by yourself.' I found a maid and she took me all over the floor and couldn't find the room either. Finally, my husband came along and told me about the change. I was relieved, I'll tell you that."

And then *it* happened. Suddenly, the entire system went haywire. Incoming calls rang in rooms that shouldn't have. Outgoing calls ceased altogether.

At six a.m., Eugene Scanlan, The Waldorf manager, was roused from a deep sleep in his suite.

Assessing the situation, he made his move. Armed with a load of dimes, he sped to the nearest phone to summon some 400 employees to the hotel. By midday there were nearly 1800 at work. Some helped at the switchboard, taking messages for guests who could not receive calls directly. Others personally delivered messages to the rooms.

Part of the fallout from the system failure was the total disruption of room service. Sunday morning breakfast and brunch orders usually keep the board buzzing.

Once again, The Waldorf resorted to complimentary lobby fare, serving free coffee, punch and pastry to those milling around. The hotel's three restaurants handled overflow crowds.

It was a hectic pace for Thomas Monetti, director of food and beverage operations. And, curiously, he found himself signalling relays of busboys to the kitchen to order more chocolate mousse, please, particularly for the afternoon crowd in Peacock Alley. "People just seem to eat more mousse in crisis situations," Mr. Monetti observed. "The same thing happened during the blackout. Maybe it's easier to spoon up than pie or cake. . ."

Mousse may be a pacifier of sorts, but everyone breathed a uniform sign of relief at the suddenly soothing sound of a ringing telephone at five p.m. that day.

A spokesman for New York Telephone Company blamed the breakdown on a failure in the computer circuit, and pointedly mentioned that over eighteen systems had been installed in the city, and "nothing has ever gone wrong during a cutover before." He added: "Unfortunately, the one time it has happened, it happened at The Waldorf. It's been no picnic, believe me".

Despite the turmoil and confusion, the press noted, most guests and staff members were "resilient and good-natured." A visiting accountant from Chicago summed up his experience: "On Friday night they shoved a nice letter under my door saying the phones were going to be changed. The next thing I knew the phones were out and there was a pleasant, well-dressed man lying on his stomach under my bed trying to fix it. It's sad in a way. You're sort of trapped in a New York hotel room without a phone. I couldn't get room service or call the theater or phone a friend. I'm not angry though. It'll pass. Everything passes."

And so it did. The night the rooms vanished and the telephones stopped ringing is now but another memory to be told and retold now and then by those who shared it.

Still, should another unexpected crisis erupt in these parts, be assured the happening may rattle the rafters, but it will scarcely ruffle the keepers of this world's most celebrated inn.

Security

TODAY'S SECURITY OFFICERS have class and style. Their manner, attire and bearing defy identity. They are often so distinguished in appearance as to blend in with the most prestigious of guests, as they patrol undetected in the hotel lobby and throughout the house. Yet their duties engulf a broader scope than that of any precinct police officer.

The Waldorf-Astoria's security force—a diligent, vigilant 24-hour squadron of men and women in plainclothes and uniforms— quietly guard eighteen entrances, forty-seven floors and corridors, a block-long lobby, a myriad of public rooms and shops and thousands of residents, transient and long-term, plus thousands more who are just passing through.

Protection of the guest is the primary concern. Sometimes, it can be routine, such as turning the knobs of doors on the post-midnight shift to make sure the sleeping occupant won't be disturbed by an unwelcome intruder. Or retrieving items which patrons regularly misplace, fear stolen or simply let slip into riddlesome regions. Countless are the calls from anguished females who have accidentally dropped rings, earrings, brooches or bracelets into the toilet bowl—and flushed! Seconds later, a reassuring security officer arrives with the handy hotel plumber in tow.

Another thorn in the security domain is the guest who declines to deposit her gems in the hotel vault, choosing to conceal them in her own ingenious hiding place. And then she forgets just where she put them! Like a scavenger hunt, the valuables turn up in the oddest places. One security officer found milady's jewels buried in the bottom of a large (and gooey) jar of cold cream. Another uncovered the missing heirlooms from the hem of the drapes; the lining seam had been slit to form a pocket.

Naturally, there are cases, too, of cunning thievery. Most brazen are the matinee burglars who cleverly coincide their capers with the guests' afternoon diversions of theater or shopping. They usually operate with stolen keys.

However, the staff is aware—and often aids in the capture.

One day, a 10th floor maid observed a well-dressed man cautiously enter and leave one suite, then another. She had never seen him before. Her suspicions aroused, she called security. A distaff detective, in chambermaid dress, was hastily dispatched to the scene. She cornered the man in question— with $6,000 worth of stolen jewelry on his person.

As a postscript to the incident, a Park Avenue matron heard about the sartorial burglar and contacted the hotel. His method, she said, appeared similar to the one used to loot her penthouse apartment. Security referred her to her local police precinct. And, when the offender's apartment was searched, police found a sizable quarry from the penthouse—a cool million-dollar collection of her valuables.

Waldorf-Astoria security officers often join forces with the New York City Police Department. Most pointedly in the protection of a visiting VIP. The amount of time and effort accorded "Operation Protection" for a visiting dignitary actually goes far beyond the few hours the luminary is in the confines of the hotel itself.

It involves weeks of planning, days of rehearsal and a mind-gripping synchronization of details. Nothing can be overlooked; the worst must be anticipated. Like a seasoned theatrical troupe, security personnel are fully prepped for opening night. Only this cast prefers to enact its drama behind the scenes, praying there will be no center stage action.

By chance, I became a participant in one major production, specifically, the delicate guarding of Margaret Thatcher, Prime Minister of Great Britain, who was being honored by the Veterans of OSS at their annual dinner held, naturally, in the grand ballroom of The Waldorf-Astoria.

OSS, the Office of Strategic Services, formed under fire in World War II, was the precursor of the Central Intelligence Agency. So, in addition to the CIA chief on the dais, many prominent intelligence figures would be in attendance.

As a vice-chairman of the OSS dinner, I was designated "coordinator of security." In that vague capacity, I was soon embroiled in the vast and intricate mechanics ensuring the safety and well-being of the Honorable Mrs. Thatcher and all those around her.

The British Information Service whetted media interest with an announcement that the Prime Minister would make an important international policy speech at the reception. The press was already spurred by the turbulent situation in Northern Ireland, where violence spread ominously as hunger strikers in the Belfast jail came near death. In New York City, volatile IRA (Irish Republican Army)

British Prime Minister Margaret Thatcher addresses a meeting of World War II O.S.S. veterans at The Waldorf.

sympathizers responded with explicit threats against the life of Mrs. Thatcher. This, then, became the backdrop for a thousand United States intelligence operatives gathered for a pleasant reunion.

As the momentum mounted, the State Department requested maximum security. And the regiments of guardian angels multiplied by the minute.

As always, when an honored guest is in the house, The Waldorf's executive staff remained on duty. The security force fanned out on patrols all over the hotel. More than 500 of the city's uniformed police barricaded four sides of the hotel, blocking fiery demonstrators from all entries. Special details of detectives canvassed the premises with trained bomb-sniffing canines. A platoon of Scotland Yard operatives joined 33 Secret Service agents for close-at-hand coverage of the Prime Minister. And I, along with every busboy, waiter and captain assigned to the banquet, underwent a strict security clearance.

However, while the ballroom contingent was being primed for elegant and precision service, I was undergoing more rigorous drills: repeated forays through the environs of the hotel, checking and double-checking every inch of carpeted acreage; monitoring, in particular, the prescribed route from the driveway entrance to The Towers suite, thence to the ballroom and back again. And again . . .

A half-hour before the reception, we stood, all of us, in position—in formal attire, a tuxedoed montage of penguins (some with bullet-proof vests and pistols at the ready). I watched the four-legged bomb squad on its final round, sniffing every inch of ballroom. Considering my own tour of duty completed, I sat down with a sigh, contemplating the pleasures of greeting OSS comrades, lifting a glass or two and indulging in cloak and dagger reminiscences, thanks to two tickets I had purchased at $75 apiece.

But, no. Secret Service advised me my job had just begun. I was to remain standing and patrol the fringes of the ballroom throughout the night. And I must remain alert (and dry!), ever watchful for any diners who might disrupt the proceedings. If that happened, I was instructed to rush to the scene, confront the offender and demand that he or she refrain or leave. If I met any resistance, Secret Service agents and police would remove the miscreant to a "holding room." After dinner, I would be called upon to file a formal complaint in the local precinct because this was a private function for which I was the official "coordinator of security."

Happily, there wasn't a single hitch in the definitively planned and rehearsed procedures. And there was no trace of any kind of unpleasant incident. The interior of The Waldorf, even with a multitude on the move, always seems to possess the rare serenity and dignity of a cathedral. Somehow you derive a feeling that the quality of its atmosphere would tone down any inspiration of turbulence.

As for Prime Minister Thatcher, she graciously accepted the OSS tribute and eloquently delivered her policy speech. An hour after the dinner ended, she was aboard her RAF plane, London bound. And the midnight detail of The Waldorf's security force resumed its routine rounds.

Fortunately, the sentinels of safety and security in the world's most celebrated hotel are well schooled in the art of guarding many of the world's most celebrated personages. And the grim assignments of tension and apprehension are balanced by episodes of humor as well.

Members of the security force chuckle when they recall the night one of their men came to the aid of a gorgeous movie doll who also happened to be an Olympic figure-skating champion and queen of the ice shows. No matter where she was or how she dressed, she was always spotted in a crowd.

On this particular evening she and I were invited to a supper club party after her ice show performance in Madison Square Garden. Sexy and healthy looking as she was, she enjoyed "cooling off" after a strenuous session on skates with lots of champagne and dancing like a dervish. I finally bid her goodnight in The Waldorf at 4:30 a.m.

She was still laughing three hours later when she phoned and awakened me to report the hilarious interlude. She had taken off her makeup, stripped and crawled between the sheets, looking forward to pleasant dreams. But sleep would not come. So she got up, switched on some soothing radio music (at low volume) and curled up nude in a wing chair, perusing a fashion magazine while hoping for the arrival of the sandman. All it induced was a drawn-out yawn.

Then she heard a muffled thud outside the door. Ah, the Sunday papers had arrived! She allowed a proper interval before she swung open her door and bent down to pick up the hefty Sunday editions of The New York Times and The Daily News.

Then it happened! The fast-closing door bumped her rump. The weight of the pile of papers in her hands propelled her into mid-corridor as the door shut resoundingly behind her. The corridor was empty. But there she was in her birthday suit, a delicately rounded, dimpled Miss Venus, size ten.

What ensued was a slapstick comedy. A door opened some forty feet away and two women emerged, on their way to early mass at St. Patrick's. With a gasp, they scrambled back to their room, phoned the desk and agitatedly described their shock at seeing a nude blonde pixie in the hall doing a Sally Rand fan dance, using the comic sheets of the newspaper instead of feathers for the peekaboo sequence.

Sure enough, when the security officer and night manager arrived with a passkey, they found the film star semi-exposed—her derriere to the door, the comic pages strategically shielding her fore. Breathlessly clutching her cartoon camouflage, she stammered her tale of woe as she mincingly retreated into her

room. The poker-faced security man thoughtfully tossed in the remaining pile of newspapers and politely saved his guffaws for the elevator.

Many of the directors of security in the hotel roster are former ranking New York City police officials and their sleuthing skills are particularly handy when it comes to salvaging the family silver—and whatever other sundries patrons decide to plunder.

The Waldorf's worldwide fame has caused it to suffer more heavily than most distinguished inns at the hands of souvenir hunters. The specifics of items pilfered are as staggering as the statistics. And the most genteel of guests can be outrageously bold in filching souvenirs.

There was the diner who was intercepted at the elevator on his way down from the Starlight Roof with an immense silver fish platter stuffed into his trousers. Security had been alerted by a watchful waiter. It was posed a problem on how to handle the situation. Do you say: "Excuse me, is that a fish platter in your pants?" Rather, the officer resorted to merely pointing to "something sticking out there and it's kind of shiny." The patron,

New York's finest provide security for a presidential visit to The Waldorf. No other national flags are flown during such a visit.

sufficiently embarrassed, submitted to the probe. As the incident was recounted, it prompted a sniff of disdain: "He didn't even bother to clean it."

Room service waiters are often conscripted to perform security tasks—simply because they must sign for every piece of costly silver they place on a table or tray. Consequently they are quick to detect a missing item. On one occasion, the waiter who called for his table at a room where an hour before he had delivered a platter of scrambled eggs noted the absence of the silver cover. He contacted security. When queried, the patron subsequently admitted he had confiscated the cover. But with an oblique explanation—his son, he said, was using it as a head protector while showering!

Even more confounding was the time a housekeeper frantically called the desk to report that a guest who just vacated a room had stripped the bathroom of everything but the tub! The assistant manager beckoned the house officer on duty in the lobby and together they tapped the culprit at the checkout counter.

The guest, an arrogant sort, exhibited arch dismay at the suggestion, voiced discreetly, that perhaps some hotel property got mixed in with his personal effects. "Would you care to examine my luggage?" he retorted.

When his bluff was called, the valise released a showcase of soft goods, from towels to bath mat to a shower curtain, still damp.

On the other side of the coin are the conscience-stricken pilferers who *return* "trophies" with touching notes of apology. Not long ago there was a rash of returns. And it all began with a package from a woman in Elizabeth, New Jersey. The note accompanying the six silver demitasse spoons recounted that the spoons were taken from the hotel thirty years ago. The occasion was a Parent-Teachers Association dinner in the grand ballroom. "Because it was my birthday," the letter writer explained, "Some of the people at the dinner decided to give me a birthday present and they filched the demitasse spoons."

Before long, she forgot about them. Then recently, she said: "With the rising price of silver, I went looking for things to dispose of and found the spoons. I am truly sorry. By nature I am an honest person."

Word of the penitent return reached the hotel's public relations office and was duly fed to the press, omitting the identity of the contrite woman. "I don't want to discourage anyone else who's honest," the P.R. director said.

Sure enough, in the months that followed an avalanche of silverware streamed back to the hotel's silver vault. Among the tide of "borrowed" silver were: some $3500 worth of spoons, two candlesticks, a candelabra, assorted ashtrays and a champagne bucket. A woman in North Carolina mailed back a silver sugar bowl stolen by her grandmother at the opening of the new Waldorf in October fifty years before. And a forty-nine-year-old silver oyster fork was personally delivered by a handsome white-haired woman who confided to the assistant manager, "I have been intending to do this for a long time."

A handwritten note accompanied another returned Waldorf heirloom: "Sorry, this has been in my silver chest for many years. I am not the culprit, but I do feel responsible to see that it is returned."

First and Foremost

FOR THREE DECADES, The Waldorf-Astoria was the largest and tallest hotel in the world. It is still the largest with its city square-block acreage and the cubic footage of its high-ceilinged rooms. And it continues to reign as flagship of the Hilton system.

It wasn't until the 1960s that a batch of new, taller inns mushroomed in midtown. However, The Waldorf's list of firsts renders it foremost in any registry.

The original Waldorf was the most innovative hostelry of its time. Many of the services and courtesies inaugurated by the old Waldorf were perpetuated in the new. And so many of them were copied, that they became standard in the industry.

It was Goerge Boldt, the original major-domo, who instituted a score of niceties that set the old Waldorf apart. He started the practice of having assistant managers in the lobby to greet and assist guests and care for their minor wants. He also put "gentlewomen" on all floors as floor clerks. He introduced room service to America. He started the "super-courtesy" idea of sending gifts, with the hotel's compliments, to prominent guests. And, he was the first to allow gentlemen to smoke in the dining rooms.

The Waldorf is recorded as the first fashionable hotel to abolish the "Ladies" entrance. And the first hotel to hire expensive orchestras for entertainment. The original Waldorf was the first to broach the subject of entertaining in a luxury hotel. It literally broke society of the habit of entertaining at home. The old Waldorf started the room and bath idea. And the new Waldorf ushered in cold water, hot water, ice water and wall receptacles for used razor blades.

Cole Porter's piano.

The new Waldorf suggested people live permanently in private hotel suites. They literally gave up their homes.

The old Waldorf was the first hotel to have a song written about it, "Meet Me at The Hyphen." The new Waldorf was the first to be lyricized in a Broadway musical. The show was "Anything Goes," the composer, Towers resident Cole Porter, and the tune, "You're The Tops." Among the comparative superlatives was the line: "You're a Waldorf salad. . ."

Another hallmark in the field of entertainment, it was the first hotel to star in a major movie production. The 1945 MGM film, "Weekend at The Waldorf," featured Ginger Rogers, Walter Pidgeon, Lana Turner and Van Johnson, with Edward Arnold, Keenan Wynn and Xavier Cugat's Orchestra thrown in. But the hotel was the star. And something of a prima donna, at that.

"On any given weekend practically anything can happen beneath the lofty towers of the fabulous Waldorf-Astoria," MGM stated in its advance publicity. And any hotel manager in America would probably have given his right eye for that kind of promotion.

But not Lucius Messinger Boomer, The Waldorf's guiding genius. Boomer took the view that Hollywood was small potatoes compared with The Waldorf-Astoria, and he almost refused to allow the picture to be made. There were things in the original script that did not conform with his idea of Waldorf ethics. And he wrote a stinging letter to the producer, Arthur Hornblow, Jr., telling him so.

The picture had been planned as a revival of "Grand Hotel," based on the best-selling Vicki Baum novel. In the 1931 film version, John Barrymore portrayed an international jewel thief who managed to get into the room of a ballet dancer, played by Greta Garbo. It also had Wallace Beery as an industrial magnate occupying a room adjoining that of his attractive secretary, a role taken by Joan Crawford.

Absolutely not! Boomer seethed. In the first place, The Waldorf would not have any international jewel thieves stopping there. (So the role was changed to a foreign correspondent.) Besides that, in his Waldorf, no man could get inside a woman's room to steal anything. (So they rewrote the script to allow Pidgeon to be wheeled accidentally into Miss Rogers' room while hiding in a linen wagon.) Furthermore, regarding the adjoining rooms of the industrial baron and his secretary . . .(In the final revision, the pretty private secretary became a public stenographer who went home after working hours.) When all alterations were made to Boomer's satisfaction, the picture was allowed to proceed.

"Weekend at The Waldorf" opened at Radio City Music Hall, where it was seen by 1,250,000 customers who waited hours in line during its nine-week run. With cinema fame, an inspired slogan swept across the nation— the dream of spending a "Weekend at The Waldorf." And, with frequent reruns on television screens, a whole new generation writes to request weekend rates. (In the Hilton tradition, children are free—even in their flagship hotel.)

As premieres go, however, no movie production could emulate the actual ribbon-cutting ceremonies for the hotel's Park Avenue opening on October 1, 1931. It was the President of the United States, Herbert Hoover, who made the inaugural toast. The Waldorf was the first and only hotel ever to merit that homage. The White House greetings were broadcast nationwide over the NBC radio network, another Waldorf first.

The Waldorf can be called the first hotel of five-star rank because it has been the residence of three five-star generals: Dwight Eisenhower, Douglas MacArthur and Omar Bradley. The five-star insignia is still displayed over a door on the seventh floor, the Eisenhower Suite.

Some of the entries in The Waldorf's book of firsts were abraded in the tides of changing times. For forty years the hotel claimed the distinction of having the only wine cellar located five floors up (to avoid the rumblings of railroad cars in the lower regions). It still does not have a "cellar" *per se*, but its reserve of fine wines and whiskeys is now kept at its proper temperatures just below street level, in the first basement.

For decades, too, the hotel could boast of the only high-in-the-sky supper club with a retractable roof. The Starlight Roof, a jewel of decor and dining, rolled back its roof from June through September to allow dancing under the stars to big name bands.

Both the Empire Room and The Starlight Roof shared the tribute of launching many of today's top entertainers. Among those who rose to stardom via The Waldorf spotlight were Dinah Shore, Victor Borge, Xavier Cugat, Edgar Bergen and Vic Damone. With the bold booking of Frank Sinatra, early in his solo fling, The Waldorf elevated the bobby-soxer's idol to swank society and international appreciation.

The late international superstar, Maurice Chevalier, provided The Waldorf with a first that few other singing entertainers would ever attempt. Can you image Lena Horne, Tony Bennett or Mick Jagger doing an entire show without one toot of music in the background? Well, the musicians' union called a

strike on the date of Chevalier's premiere in the Empire Room. The Frenchman volunteered with that show-must-go-on spirit. If he had a 50-piece symphony behind him, the audience could not have appreciated his performance more. He was magnificent.

The advent of air-conditioning induced the permanent closing of the rooftop and lost the charm of open air, moonlight and stars. Nevertheless, the Starlight Roof remains today one of the most fascinating settings as a ballroom or banquet room.

The staggering salaries that Miami Beach and then Las Vegas came to pay solo stars of the entertainment world made it unreasonable, indeed impossible, for New York hotels to compete for headliners. So The Waldorf introduced another first, more intimate entertainment. Now, in Peacock Alley or Hideaway or wherever the festive crowd happens to be gathering, you will find an entertainer at a piano.

Certain firsts, however, remain forever intact. For instance, the Art Deco grandeur of The Waldorf's architecture is permanently embedded in the hotel's walls, ceilings and accessories. The hotel is not only a masterpiece rendition of the period but is considered an Art Deco museum. Tours are conducted outside as well as within the hotel. It is known as "the Art Deco building" and guides point out the Pompeian columns of Rockwood stone standing two by two beneath a gold and silver leaf plaster ceiling; the pillars of rouge marble; the paneled walls of burled walnut inlaid with ebony; the motifs of urns and garlands and baskets of flowers superimposed on latticework of nickel and bronze. It is an artistic treasury of design and gilt. And it remains for all to see and marvel.

Some of The Waldorf firsts are simply a reflection of the hotel's inimitable hospitality and warmth of attitude towards its guests.

The Waldorf was the first to set up Seder tables in the lobby at the Jewish holiday of Passover. And it was the first hotel to conduct a Christmas service in its lobby. It was on the snowy morning of December 25, 1978, that an interdenominational service was held. That eclectic celebration included a children's group in colonial costumes, a "Yankee Tunesmith Fife and Drum Corps" and a traditional choir. All of this took place in the ornate Park Avenue lobby, which was also graced by a Hanukkah menorah.

At one time, The Waldorf contained so many extraordinary features that it was said that a child could be brought to life and grow up within its domain and never have to step outdoors.

The Waldorf was also the first to have professional guides on its staff. Among the hotel's myriad of conveniences there was even a fully equipped mini-hospital and dental offices. One guide was askance when a former president of Mexico, General Plutarco Calles, after viewing The Waldorf hospital, asked to be shown "The Waldorf's private cemetery."

The most unusual first? It must have been the birthday party staged for the first lady of the land—in The Waldorf's garage!

Hundreds of employees and officers of the hotel assembled with balloons, candles, a birthday cake and a musical chorus in the

Then First Lady Betty Ford's birthday inspired one of The Waldorf's most unusual surprise parties, staged in the hotel's garage by Waldorf employees to greet her as she arrived at the limousine entrance.

driveway. When President Gerald Ford's limousine arrived at The Waldorf's central underpass, out stepped Betty Ford—to the biggest birthday surprise of her life!

As the MGM advertisements said, "Anything can happen beneath the lofty towers of the fabulous Waldorf-Astoria." And does.

And, finally, The Waldorf holds title to this unique claim: it is the only inn to receive any mail simply addressed: "Best Hotel, New York." The letters are delivered without question by the post office.

And who can argue with that?

114

From Kitchens to Tables

THE WALDORF KITCHEN IS sweet to the scent and deafening to the ears. It's a remarkable operation of efficiency and chaos, where order somehow manages to reign above the clatter of china, the din of pots and pans, the quick slip and the fast mop-up, and the rapid-fire cries of waiters and busboys on the run.

The food that is daily ordered and stored, in the freezer, refrigerator, chiller or pantry, can feed a small army. More than two million meals a year are served in The Waldorf-Astoria. Guests in a typical day consume 12,000 rolls, 10,000 eggs, 6,000 pounds of prime beef, 2,750 pounds of striped bass, 2,400 Rock Cornish hens, 1,000 pounds of string beans, 200 lobsters and 1,000 gallons of coffee.

Nearly a thousand employees are engaged in the split-second stewardship of dispensing food and beverages. One man does nothing but squeeze fresh orange juice all day.

Another chops parsley. Four men make nothing but coffee. Six men spend all day polishing silver.

The main kitchen occupies the entire second floor of the building, the equivalent of a city square block. The hotel also has a separate kitchen for room service. A third floor banquet kitchen caters to the Grand Ballroom, serving as many as 1,600 persons at one time, and there are satellite kitchens geared to the functions of the adjacent Jade and Astor Salons.

A fifth kitchen, for intimate banquets, is located on the fourth floor. And a sixth cookery is high in the sky on the 18th floor, next to the famous Starlight Roof, preparing party fare for 650 persons or more.

Then there are the restaurant kitchens: one for the Bull and Bear, one for Oscar's and a third serving continental cuisine for both Peacock Alley and the private Marco Polo Club.

Finally, there is a separate kitchen and dining room for "The Waldorf Family." It is called The Outer World and it offers a bounty of "three squares" for all employees on the third floor rear.

On a normal day, all ten kitchens are humming at full staff, grinding out gourmet fare for the out-of-town guest, the on-the-town host, visiting VIPs and the in-house "family." To a visitor, a curious outsider, observing the frenzied, but precise performance, it is a mind-boggling, cymbal-clashing scene of perpetual motion.

"How does it work?" I wonder aloud.

"It's teamwork!" a junior chef sings out. "We're a baseball team. Everybody plays his position, so everything runs smoothly."

We tour the stations, designated by signs. Fish. Soup. Sauce. Roast. Garde Manger. . .

We pass barrels of potatoes, crates of carrots, bins of onions. And pause, mesmerized by the warm, batter-sweet redolence of the pastry shop. Here is the huge European brick oven, "never turned off." Here is where the famous macaroons are baked—2,000 a day, the trademark cookie from the old Waldorf days. President Lyndon Johnson had a habit of stuffing them in his pocket, we are told, much to the dismay of Ladybird.

And here is where the famous Waldorf wedding cakes are created; sometimes eight tiers high, sometimes taller than the bridal couple—fifty man-hours to make.

The bakers are artists; their skills pleasing to the eye as well as the palate. A Bengal prince once gave the kitchen a photograph of his bejeweled turban. The Waldorf reproduced it—a delicious replica with frosted jewels in sugared icing.

At the soup station, specialists labor over cauldrons of cream of tomato, oyster chowder or consomme of chicken. One assembles the ingredients, another is occupied solely with skimming, a third does the clarification, a fourth is the taster.

To make the marvelous sauces, there is a saucier and four or five helpers. A friturier (fry cook) keeps the oil sizzling in huge iron pots and pans for the crisping of French fried potatoes, the sautéing of scallops, the dipping of cream puffs. . .

In the butcher shop, one man cuts chickens, another slices meat. All of the meat arrives fresh, in primary cuts; the butcher chops it to portion size, trims the fat and prepares it for broiling or roasting—and service on a silver platter.

In the cold room, an ice-cream chef chisels an eagle from ice . . .

And in the area of garde manger, a delicately proportioned woman creates flowers from raw vegetables and all varieties of hors d'oeuvres.

The garde manger also dresses fowl and fish for the fire and prepares cold dishes for buffets. Here partridges are bathed in Bordeaux, rubbed with herbs and stuffed with paté de foie gras. And here a staff of twenty slices a turkey, then builds a scaffold of toothpicks on the carcass, so it can be re-

A reception in The Waldorf's Basildon Room.

117

formed for display on the tables. They are architects and sculptors who can make fountains of cold lobsters—or platters of tasty tidbits.

Elsewhere, in the pantries, a corps of men and women are scooping melons and slicing fruits; stripping leaves of lettuce—to mix with chicory, romaine, escarole and endives—for thousands of bib and greengrocer salads.

There is always action in The Waldorf kitchens. It's a round-the-clock production of preparation, cooking, serving and cleaning. But the momentum reaches a peak crescendo at banquet time.

The first banquet ever held in a hotel was in the old Waldorf in 1893. Ever since, The Waldorf has reigned supreme in that domain. More banquets are held in The Waldorf-Astoria than any other hotel in the world. And of the more than $30 million in annual revenue tabbed by the food and beverage department, fifty percent is derived from the business of banquets.

An average of 28 functions per day are held in the 24 public rooms. And, with a staff of experts, long in experience, each Waldorf-Astoria reception, large or small, is a masterpiece of perfection, a clockwork gem of food and service.

It is particularly impressive in the setting of the magnificent Grand Ballroom. The only two-tiered ballroom in the city, this sumptuous space is between the third and seventh floors, with an area 135 feet long and 120 feet wide beneath the festooned balconies. It has all the elegance and splendor of an 18th century Versailles, adorned with gilt and murals, a spectacular crystal chandelier ten feet in diameter), mirrored insets and velvet swashes.

But when the dinner gong chimes, it strikes the military regimen of a 20th century space program . . .

The kitchen doors swing to and fro as waiters and busboys march in and out. They proceed in prescribed order, follow-the-leader style. There is no colliding or tilting of trays. They are an army of regulars, rigorously trained in their maneuvers.

Rehearsals begin early in the day, while other workers are readying the room for the scheduled feast. A brigade of decorators drape the balconies, garland the columns. Men and women scrub and polish the brass railings. Sweepers and dusters clean chairs and boxes. Carpets, curtains and canopies are made spic and span. The stage is set for hundreds of tables to be rolled in, set up with linen cloths, china, stemware and polished silverware. Florists arrive with fresh flowers, leaves vividly green.

The secret of The Waldorf's banquet success is as much timing as tempting dishes. For sometimes the occupancy of the room juggles the set-up schedule, allowing minutes rather than hours for preparation for the next function.

A typical example is the annual conclave of the National Association of Manufacturers. Some 1,800 members gathered for the meeting in the main ballroom from 10 a.m. to noon. Luncheon was scheduled for 12:30 p.m.

The half hour between the adjournment of the meeting and the formal luncheon could have been a rest or wash-up period for the members. Instead, the majority gathered in the balcony boxes, enthralled with the swift-paced procedure taking place below.

And when lunch ended, promptly at 2 p.m., members repositioned themselves in their viewing perches for the twenty minutes it took to restore the room as meeting quarters. Afterwards, some strays remained to watch the final transition for the 6:30 p.m. dinner. "Best show in town!" a lingering spectator commented.

In its time, the Grand Ballroom has been the scene of historic occasions. Kings and queens, presidents and prime ministers have been feted there and delivered momentous messages. It has been the site of the foremost

At work in the kitchens.

A Waldorf dinner honoring philanthropist Charles Silver (LEFT) brings together John F. Kennedy, the late Archbishop of New York Francis Cardinal Spellman and Richard M. Nixon.

social, civic and political galas of the past fifty years. Entire Broadway productions have appeared on its mammoth stage.

It has also hosted events not usually associated with ballrooms: The enormous "auto" elevator behind the Grand Ballroom has borne cars for the General Motors Auto Show; animals for a barnyard party—a live collection of chickens, ducks, pigs, cows and donkeys (fitted with felt shoes to protect the polished floors); circus elephants for an Elsa Maxwell shindig (Dorothy Kilgallen quipped, "Which one is the elephant?" and Elsa never spoke to her again); and twelve huge Clydesdale horses for a brewing company celebration.

The Waldorf carpenters always rose to the occasion, plying their tools to help house decorators convert the ballroom to whatever theme was mandated.

The Waldorf electricians worked overtime setting up for the memorable Pillsbury Bake-Off, an annual contest in which one hundred stoves were installed on the ballroom floor and flour clouded the air as contestants feverishly competed for the crown. The winner received cash, the runners-up a four-day stay at The Waldorf. And when the last cookie and fruited or nutted concoction was whisked from the ovens, the last morsel tasted by the panel of judges, the stoves were hastily removed, the baking vessels returned to the kitchen and the room was transformed to a banquet setting for the scheduled evening dinner.

While the efficiency and production of the hotel's banquet department can be dramatically perceived by the public, there is a vital branch of the routine feeding of thousands of guests that is seldom seen but equally impressive.

Behind the scenes, 24 hours a day, room service answers the calls of hungry guests. From a telecommunication center in a booth off the second floor kitchen, seven sentries record and dispatch orders. There may be some 500 to 700 requests for breakfast (anything from the standard orange juice, eggs, toast and coffee to a hearty steak-and-potatoes morning meal). The food arrives within minutes—in heated vessels, on tables draped in yellow linen, with bud vases and fresh flowers.

Room service also harkens to the hunger pangs of a guest who hankers for a grilled Reuben sandwich in the wee hours of two or three a.m. And room service is the caterer to fancy dinner parties given by swank hosts and hostesses in their Tower suites. The Towers residents may use their own tableware and butlers, but they rely on room service to provide the elaborate menu and divine fare.

Although the majority of guests relish breakfast in bed, or elsewhere in their suites, there are many who prefer the garden setting of Oscar's or the rosy-hued Peacock Alley. Both restaurants are open for customers at 7 a.m.

Henry Kissinger, an early riser, was a morning regular in Peacock Alley. So are many of the hotel's corporate executive neighbors, along with early-bird tourists eager to hit the town.

"The Waldorf is probably the only hotel where 75 percent of the restaurant business comes from local residents," notes Thomas Monetti, director of food and beverage operations. And, in the inherent tradition of this grand hotel, "All guests are treated as VIPs."

Each of The Waldorf restaurants has a personality of its own. Any variation of prices has more to do with the ambiance and menu selection than the quality of cuisine.

The salads, vegetables and baked goods are the same. However, Peacock Alley may feature: "Medallions of Beef Tenderloin, Sliced Artichokes, Mustard Seeds, Cognac, Dash of Cream and Veal Glaze. Prepared by Your Captain. 23." There are no dollar signs on Waldorf menus. But the Bull and Bear may offer "Oxford John—A Durham Beef Stew with Vegetables" or "Saddle of Down Lamb, Roast Potato and Green Beans, Mint Jelly" (both $16.25) to its predominantly male customers.

Although it is now coed (and is duly described as "The Men's Restaurant that Women Love"), the Bull and Bear retains the masculine trappings of its former title: The Men's Bar. It was built after Repeal, a leathery retreat that was a throwback to the old Waldorf, with an African mahogany reproduction of the fabulous four-sided bar that was deemed a quadrangular annex of Wall Street. The menu carried the legend, "At the sign of the Bull and Bear." And the bronze statues brought over from the original Waldorf reinforced the slogan. They also electrified the old gas fixture and hung it over the new bar.

The scions of industry and finance made the new surroundings their "club" in the same manner as their forebears. Some new faces joined the ranks in addition to such familiar patrons as Henry Luce, Roy Howard, Beardsley Ruml, Alfred Gwynne Vanderbilt and Emerson Foote. Waiters rated each gourmet in the best tradition, "A man who knows how to eat and demands that it be cooked just so."

Today's regulars form a grand old guard. They are issued personal monogrammed glasses and membership cards: "For those who have developed the technique to toss the

Bull, and those who have the patience to stand there and Bear it."

While women may enjoy the liberation of libation with males in the Bull and Bear, there is no disputing that for courtship any man can surely captivate his lady fair in the enchanted atmosphere of the pastel Peacock Alley. All pink and green, floral and candlelit, with a tinkling piano, and genteel waiters bowing and attending.

The Waldorf waiter is a special breed. He, too, is a hallmark of tradition. A reminder of standards set long ago. My favorite recollection in this sphere concerns the lectures delivered by my dear friend, Rene Black. A colorful, erudite, sophisticated artist (he would sketch on menus for guests), the mustachioed Rene served as chief of restaurants and tutor *par excellence* for The Waldorf waiters.

With the oratorical bearing of a William Jennings Bryan, he would conduct seminars two or three times a week. Black set the tone with such bon mots as: "We must create the service of good cuisine instead of hashing." Then he would eloquently boost his staff's status: "If you feel that the world looks down on a waiter, then you are no waiter. You are a hash slinger. . .A waiter's profession, when it is properly understood, is just as important a position as one in medicine, or science, or literature."

The Waldorf's Peacock Alley is a popular meeting place.

In clipped syllables, he would elaborate: "I don't expect a waiter to know the circumference of the globe, but food relates to all sorts of knowledge. He must be ready to answer the patron who asks: Truffles? Where do they come from? Where do they find artichokes in the United States?"

Oral exams followed the pep talk: "How do you make filet of sole Winterthur? Why was this dish created? For whom was it created? Today we have on the menu Brochette Bersane. If anybody who can tell me what it is, I'll give him $5."

In The Waldorf code, a waiter must never carry a towel under his arm, or gather with other waiters to talk in the dining room, or snap his fingers to attract a busboy or show disappointment about the size of his tip.

The rules and rigors of The Waldorf kitchen are similarly explicit: salads must be done freshly and served crisp. Pâté de foie gras must be served on a plate that is ice cold, not lukewarm. Oysters cannot be opened at seven when dinner is at nine. A thick soup must be made very hot before incorporating the cream; otherwise the cream will curdle.

In charge of the kitchen and all its rudiments is a man who has served at every kitchen station in the past forty-plus years. Executive Chef Kurt Ermann, born in Germany and schooled in France, arrived on these shores on the Queen Mary, July 4, 1938. Four days later he was "second cook" at a Lake Placid resort. After Labor Day, he joined The Waldorf staff as chef poissoniere ("preparer of fish and fish sauces").

"I wanted always to come to The Waldorf," Ermann exudes. "From the beginning, I was so proud to be of The Waldorf. The Waldorf kitchen was always tops, the top of the Escoffier. We still keep up with the Escoffier."

With a toss of his head, topped by the high white chef's chapeau, he exclaims: "The Waldorf is the finest cooking. And it makes the finest cooks. But," he shrugs, "then they leave to go to different hotels. We keep training and teaching."

Chefs at work in The Waldorf kitchens (PHOTO: MATTHEW MAURO).

For Kurt, The Waldorf kitchen is his soul and sustenance. In more than four decades of "unlimited hours" (interrupted only by a World War II army tour), he has been sous chef (assistant) to every executive chef, and relief chef on every station.

From its inception 20 years ago, Ermann has cooked for the private Marco Polo Club and prepared the annual banquet for The Explorers Club, creating exotic delicacies from wild boar, hippopotamus, rattlesnake, North African sheep—whatever the adventurous members supplied for the feast.

And, proudly, "I was cooking for every U.S. President since I came over."

In 1981, Kurt was named executive chef.

The appointment coincided with the golden anniversary of The Waldorf-Astoria. And Ermann was delighted that he would be in charge of the cuisine for the auspicious champagne reception held in the Grand Ballroom on the eve of the fiftieth anniversary, September 30, 1981.

The menu (originally estimated for 1,800, expanded to 2,500 because of early departures and late arrivals) was a dramatic melange of outstanding dishes prepared for the famous world figures who had stayed at the hotel since its Park Avenue opening in 1931.

The buffet selections included: Goujonettes of Fresh Trout rolled in Corn Meal (as served to President Herbert Hoover) . . .Brochettes of Sweet & Sour Pork (as served to the King and Queen of Siam in the Thirties) . . . Mushrooms Farci (as served to President Franklin Delano Roosevelt) . . . Cornets of York Ham (as served to Winston Churchill in the Forties) . . . Tartelettes of Seafood Americaine (as served to His Eminence Francis Cardinal Spellman) . . . Smoked Icelandic Salmon (as served to Queen Elizabeth and The Duke of Edinburgh in the Fifties) . . . Rondelles of Pâté (as served to Princess Grace of Monaco) . . . Country Ballontine of Chicken (as served to His Holiness Pope Paul VI in the Sixties) . . . Honey Dipped Southern Fried Chicken Tidbits (as served to President Jimmy Carter) . . . Kabobs of Lamb (as served to King Hussein of Jordan in the Seventies) . . . Jelly Beans (as enjoyed by President and Mrs. Ronald Reagan) . . . Miniature Pirojkes (as served to Mayor Edward Koch and the 23

OVERLEAF: A huge birthday cake dominates the ballroom at The Waldorf's 50th anniversary party (PHOTO: MATTHEW MAURO).

The Waldorf's chefs and their staffs pose proudly behind some of their creations.

Mrs. Douglas MacArthur, Barron Hilton and Ginger Rogers join in the ceremonial cutting of the first slice of The Waldorf's birthday cake (PHOTO: MATTHEW MAURO).

American ex-hostages of Iran and their families during the Eighties).

As a vote of confidence in The Waldorf's future, a table was designated: "The Year 2000 and Beyond" with such delicacies as Marinated Harvest Moon Vegetables, Saucer of Abalone with Stardust, Solar Rays of Waters Nature and A Composition of Planetary & Universal Nuts à la Chef Kurt.

The reception, of course, was a tremendous success. Champagne flowed from seven double bars set up in the main ballroom, the east and west foyers, and the first tier of the balcony.

Spotlighted in the center of the ballroom was a 15-foot-square platform, two feet high, topped by a birthday cake large enough to make the *Guinness Book of Records*. The cake had a big candle on top, but the terraced cake rose so high that lighting the candle became a serious problem at the last minute.

In the nick of time, someone came up with a bright idea. An emergency call to St. Patrick's Cathedral did the trick. An envoy was dispatched to the church to borrow its tallest candle lighter-snuffer, the instrument an altar boy must use to light the topmost candles in the cathedral.

It was an evening to remember. And Executive Chef Kurt was among those who glowed with pride and lifted his glass to "The Next Fifty Years."

Keeping the House Clean

THE COURTYARD OF THE All Day Children's School was crowded with mothers coming to pick up their young. Among them was Liesa Segovia. As she spotted her blonde five-year-old Katya, she waved and spread her arms.

A woman, standing alongside, eyed her appraisingly. "Your daughter tells me you are a housekeeper. Is that true?"

Liesa shrugged. "Yes, basically, that's right . . ."

"I did not want to get into a long discussion," Liesa remarked as she recalled the incident.

So she left out the details.

The fact is, Liesa Segovia is director of housekeeping services at The Waldorf-Astoria, in charge of 1,852 rooms—their care, repair, decoration, redecoration and daily supplies—plus all public space, including the sidewalks.

As executive housekeeper, she heads The

Waldorf's largest department, overseeing a staff of 400, including 12 in her office, 22 day floor housekeepers, four night housekeepers, 154 day maids (in charge of 12 rooms each), 17 bath maids (they do bathrooms only), 24 night maids (they do 50 "turndowns," leaving a lace doily with a chocolate mint and a pleasant dreams message on every pillow), three lobby maids and four parlor maids (for the function rooms).

In addition, there is a separate staff for The Towers: four housekeepers, 35 day maids, eight night maids (60 "turndowns" each) and six bath maids (who also clean pantries and kitchens).

Plus 64 housemen, including seven wall washers, eight window washers, furniture polishers, carpet repairmen, 31 night sanitation workers and rubbish collectors and four men who sweep the sidewalks and gutters around the entire block.

In her linen room, 20 men and women sort and weigh the laundry that comes zooming down the chutes every morning. Nearby, five seamstresses keep sewing machines humming, repairing linens and uniforms.

Then there is a woman who does nothing else but stitch burns in the hotel's plush Austrian-tufted carpeting. Counting stairwells, The Waldorf lobby rug covers a square city block. It is trod upon by one and a half million people yearly. The fallout is a massive mess of cinder spots caused by the careless flicking of ashes and grinding of cigars and cigarettes underfoot.

The carpet-burns specialist carries threads of many colors. And, as she makes her rounds, on her knees, inspecting and repairing, there are, to be sure, curious reactions. Management gets frequent calls reporting: "There's a strange woman crawling around the lobby . . ." When her behavior is explained, the caller is usually contrite—and impressed.

The Waldorf's east bank of elevators never stop at the fifth floor. And those who work in or visit the vast housekeeping headquarters either walk down one flight from the sixth floor or up one flight from the fourth. The skipped elevator stop keeps strays away. It also keeps the executive housekeeper hopping just a little bit more.

Her daily rounds begin in the linen room, which could easily stock Bloomingdale's and then some. Here are the tablecloths and napkins, coded by color: beige for the Bull and Bear, shadow rose for Peacock Alley, gold for room service, maple sugar for Marco Polo, plus aisles of blue and red and pink and gold and white for banquets.

Piles and piles of sheets and pillow cases are carted to each floor linen closet. Two pillows for every bed, three sheets for every mattress. The Waldorf has a three-sheet tradition: one for the mattress, one under the blanket, one *over* the blanket, followed by the bedspread. The third sheet is to protect the blanket—and those who may be allergic to wool.

Another Waldorf tradition is the hand-stitched Irish linen face towels. "I believe we are the only hotel to still use these towels," the housekeeper notes. "They must be reordered annually—a year in advance. With The Waldorf crest." Every bathroom is stocked with four terry bath towels, four linen face towels, a bathmat and three washcloths, fresh daily and all white.

Pleasing VIPs is routine at The Waldorf and a specialty of the executive housekeeper. She keeps an amenity closet filled with a select supply of choice china, porcelain, blankets, crib bumpers, linen and sundries known to be preferred by heads of state or industry, diplomats or royalty who may drop in unexpectedly.

Tucked among the ceiling-high amenity shelves are green towels embossed "Le Barron" and yellow for "La Barronesse"—should the Hilton Hotels president and his wife stop by for a night or two. Also, rose towels with the initials "NR" and beige with "RR"— ready for a visit from President Ronald and Nancy Reagan, who have always stayed at

Former President Gerald Ford with First Lady Nancy Reagan and President Ronald Reagan at a Waldorf function.

The Waldorf on New York visits—even before the White House.

"Nancy likes red," the housekeeper noted. "But bright red didn't go with the Presidential Suite bathroom scheme, so we settled for a soft rose."

The first lady also posed a problem for the room service caterers. She informed them she preferred place mats to tablecloths. Housekeeping immediately purchased white linen placemats embroidered with flowers. Word also spread that this was the first Presidential couple to request breakfast in bed.

The hotel's amenity closet still has dozens of "LBJ" towels—yellow linen, monogrammed in blue—reminders of the late President Lyndon Johnson and his Ladybird. And former President Gerald Ford continues to make The Waldorf his New York headquarters. So there's a score of amenities set aside for him. "There's Ford's teakettle, Betty's porcelain boudoir dish and a special crystal ashtray for his pipe," the housekeeper pointed out.

Then she produced a pair of framed Ford family portraits, which are set upon the dresser and living room table in his seventh floor suite prior to his arrival. "Just some homey touches," the housekeeper commented.

There are other distinctive facets of Towers housekeeping. The last thing a Towers maid does after cleaning is to carpet sweep her footsteps. Also, after the cigarette urns near the elevators are cleaned—three times daily—the Waldorf seal is pressed into the sands of each urn.

Housekeeping takes inventory every three months; purchasing must be done a year in advance. Sometimes it's little things, like 40,000 boxes of tissues or 60,000 hangers (including skirt hangers for the ladies, pants hangers for men and satin hangers for The Towers).

And sometimes it's big, like entire floors of new furniture. For housekeeping is also decorating and "rehab." "Rehab" is short for rehabilitation and the hotel annually redecorates some 250 rooms, floor to ceiling, wall to wall.

On one typical day, the executive housekeeper paced the length of the 17th floor —undergoing "rehab"—with clipboard in hand, beeper attached to her belt, gingerly stepping over wires, furniture, paint pails and tools. Everywhere she went she was hailed with workmen's requests and complaints:

"That window in 1746 just broke . . ."

"I'll get the window people . . ."

"There are 22 pieces of furniture sitting on the platform, where do we put 'em?"

"Have them brought up, I'll show you . . ."

From a hall phone, she dials more directions: "Send up the shades for 1756 . . . I need someone to fix the toilet paper roll in 1742 . . ."

She issues a frantic cry to the crew: "Remember! Everything must be ready by Saturday!"

Then she scoots down the stairs for a thorough inspection of the 16th floor. "Would you believe this looked like the floor above just a week ago?"

The 84 rooms are shipshape. She notes: "Color schemes, furnishings, wallpaper, carpeting, curtains, everything carefully selected and blended by the most famous interior decorators in the country."

Now it's up and around to a 39th floor Towers suite being refurnished by a "big name" decorator. Two assistants are installing drapes in the mirrored and gray-papered dining room. "Oh, I like the tassels," she comments. Then her voice takes on a cautionary tone: "You must be finished by two p.m. tomorrow. The Japanese Foreign Minister is due to arrive by four."

Next, she heads for the upholstery shop on the 43rd floor, in search of a small settee sent up for repair. In this habitat of wooden frames and bolts of material, work tables and sewing machines, a corner area is set aside for two men who do nothing but "take care of shades and shirred curtains."

The beeper sounds now, beckoning her back to her office. On the way, she inspects light fixtures in the elevators, peruses corridors, pausing often to bend and pick up a stray piece of paper or thread or lint. Everywhere she walks, the executive housekeeper moves her hands like a mother-in-law examining for dust, an area glossed over by a maid who will later be reprimanded.

"In a house this big, with a staff this large, there must be discipline," the chief nods, with a military snap of her head. However, the discipline may lag a bit in her own domestic quarters. "I don't have the time to clean my own apartment," she wails.

And it's difficult, too, for the "live-in housekeeper" to curb the adventurous spirit of her pixieish daughter. "Everyone knows Katya. And many spoil her. The maids, the doormen, they're all her friends. She loves living here. And she can't understand the reaction at school when they ask her where she lives and she tells them: 'At The Waldorf!'"

They may have read *Eloise at the Plaza* but they are unfamiliar with "Katya at the Waldorf." Few are aware, for instance, of Katya's initial impact upon the hotel. Mother and child moved into their suite the night of October 16, 1980. Liesa remained with her daughter all night in the new surroundings. Both expressed pleasure in the beauty, comfort and excitement of their nice new home.

The next night, however, Liesa tucked Katya in bed, waited until she had fallen asleep, then went on duty. "All department heads are on duty when heads of state are in the house."

And, on October 17th, an incumbent president and a possible future president were on the premises. The hotel was saturated with security guards, secret service and New York City police.

It was the night of the Alfred E. Smith Dinner, always a draw for the big politicians, a must for the mayor, the governor, senators and congressmen; and particularly important this presidential election year because President Jimmy Carter and Republican candidate Ronald Reagan were appearing together, on the dais, for the first time.

In the flurry of hotel preparations, Mrs. Segovia had not yet received her beeper nor did she get the keys to her office. While making her rounds, she paused on the fifth floor and heard a phone ringing in her office. She tried the door. It was locked. So she went to the lobby, en route to the manager.

"It was a mob scene, wall-to-wall people," she recalls. "Men and women in formal dress, police in uniform, hotel staff and guards. Suddenly, I stopped short. I could not believe my eyes. There, in a chair next to the assistant manager's desk sat this little blonde girl in her underwear and pajama top. It was Katya. She had been awakened by the sirens and commotion and she wanted to see what all the fuss was about."

Liesa shook her head. "The assistant manager explained he had tried to reach me and I explained about the keys."

"Anyway, I scooped her up in my arms and carried her off. I remember a lot of people smiling, but my heart was beating so fast. I thought: This is my first night on the job in this wonderful hotel; will it be my last?"

Somehow the incident was never recorded or reported. And somehow the pair settled down to hotel life in their cozy nest on the thirteenth floor west. In time, the precocious tyke would merely chatter away at breakfast with a casual: "Mom, is there anybody important in the house today?"

Being a live-in housekeeper has its advantages: "I'm right here in case . . ." And its disadvantages: "I'm always here in case . . ." But one thing is certain—keeping the house in order at The Waldorf-Astoria is never dull!

"You never know what famous person will be dropping in. You never know what historic events will be taking place here. And you never know what will need fixing that day." She smiled. "It's hard to explain, but I love it. We love it."

And how do you explain all that to another mother you meet outside of a school who asks if you really are a . . . housekeeper?

Keeping the Flags
Flying

I WAS HALFWAY THROUGH this book, an all-encompassing labor of love, when I chanced upon an old buddy, a former manager of The Waldorf who is now president of one of Atlantic City's most extravagant hotel casinos.

For an hour or so, we compared fond reminiscences and I detailed some chapters I had written. It was then he posed the zinger, "Have you explored the flag room?"

"Flag room?" I echoed rhetorically. Was it a restaurant, supper club or a private rendezvous of yesteryear?

He shook his head disdainfully. "Are you putting me on? The Waldorf's flag room is one of a kind. It has the largest single collection of flags in all hoteldom. It matches the United Nations'. In fact, if the UN is stuck—its pennant on loan or getting cleaned—it simply borrows from The Waldorf."

I nodded. Of course, I was aware of The Waldorf flags tradition. How many times had I paused at the hotel entrance to shade my eyes as I gazed skyward to see what flags were flying that day, denoting who was in the house—and in what order of distinction.

I had known, for instance, that protocol priority dictated primary position on Park Avenue, secondary on Lexington Avenue, tertiary on East 49th Street.

Who determines the protocol of pennant display? And how accurate is he?

Well, there was this passage in a Broadway play called "Give 'em Hell Harry." It dealt with the ruminations of a feisty Missourian, Harry S. Truman, when he occupied the Oval Office. One day a Truman aide was baffled as to which flag to display at the White House. Harry counseled him laconically to call The Waldorf-Astoria in New York because they had a protocol chief who knew all about these things. One more example of the deferential regard with which America's unofficial palace is held!

The flag room is no musty attic. It is a museum of sorts, tucked away on the 49th Street side of the hotel, a floor above The Hideaway (the intimate oasis "hidden" in the south wing of the lobby).

In these cloistered quarters are housed one of the world's most imposing collections of flags. These are flags of every nation on earth plus the flags of the United States President and Vice President, the State of New York, the City of New York, the Cardinal Archbishop of New York, the Pope and assorted organizations of note.

Numbering nearly four hundred, including duplicates (allowing for repair and cleaning as well as replacement), the big flags are twelve by eighteen feet each. And there are smaller editions (three by five feet) designed to be flown outside The Towers entrance when heads of state are in the house. It's a veritable swarm of flapping flags atop The Towers marquee when the United Nations is in session!

The flags are hoisted each morning before seven a.m. and ceremoniously lowered before sunset. Only the Park Avenue flags are flown

day and night, illuminated after dark by two powerful beams atop the entrance marquee. The Park Avenue buntings are also flown in wet weather as well as dry.

One of the major problems the flag-keepers face is keeping the banners dry. To combat destructive mildew, they are routinely given a spin in the hotel's dryer. When soiled or weather-beaten, they are sent out for dry cleaning. Another quandary is the hoisting of a flag of horizontal stripes without emblem. It's so easy to unfurl it upside down. On a vessel at sea or anywhere else in the world, an upside-down flag is an international signal of distress.

When this happens (in rare instances), the telephone room vibrates with the buzz of vituperative nationals of the country concerned. It's hard to fathom how a small country can have so many citizens in Manhattan awake at that early hour—and within view of their nation's colors—to react so alarmingly to their flag hanging in the SOS distress position.

It is a curious note, too, to reflect upon the volatile reactions expressed when international courtesy or protocol dictates the unfurling of the crimson symbol of the Union of Soviet Socialist Republics. There is something about the sight of the hammer and sickle that ignites the partisans of the American Legion, the Veterans of Foreign Wars, the Military Order of World Wars and various anti-Communist alliances. Like bulls fomented by a whirling red cape, they bristle with fury. First the irate phone calls, then the pickets of protest. And, finally, from the screwball fringe, the stream of bomb threats.

As an historic footnote, the Nazi swastika once (and only once) was unfurled from the Waldorf mast—on the day of the landing of the Graf Zeppelin and the honoring of its skipper, Dr. Hugo Eckener.

In addition to paying tribute to VIPs in residence, Waldorf flags are flown for holidays of every friendly nation. And warm notes of gratitude acknowledge this thoughtful salute.

The busiest flag in the storeroom is Japan's. It seems there is always some Nipponese nobleman or minister pausing in The Towers. There is also the square footage in the hotel occupied by the Bank of Tokyo (on Park Avenue) and the Inagiku Restaurant (the only U.S. branch) located on 49th Street. So, on the extremely rare days when there are fewer than three specific flag requisites, up goes the pennant of the Rising Sun.

The Stars and Stripes, of course, are always displayed on all sides of the hotel. And if the President of the United States is on the premises, no foreign flags are flown.

The cost of maintaining its distinction as the number one flag waver in the nation can be rather staggering. The tab for foreign flags is $875 per. The plentiful supply of Stars and Stripes runs $250 apiece. And special identity flags—carrying the seals of the President, the Vice President, the Pope and others—top $1000 each.

Two special identity flags, extremely expensive, are now obsolete. One was a red flag with gold border and a circle of five large white stars in its center. It was flown in honor of five-star generals such as Douglas MacArthur, Dwight Eisenhower and Omar Bradley when they were in residence. The last to die was Bradley.

The other five-star, gold-rimmed flag had a field of Navy blue. In our armed forces, there are no longer any admirals of five-star rank.

On June 9, 1976, the telephone room at The Waldorf hummed like a hive of hornets. Hundreds of callers wanted to know why the flags on Park Avenue were flying at half-mast. Operators explained that this was in final tribute to a beloved resident of the hotel who had passed away, the illustrious former Postmaster General James A. Farley, Sr.

Such singular respectful honors were accorded to few others in the hotel's history. The colors were dipped in 1964 to mark the death of former President Herbert Hoover, who had made The Towers his home upon his leaving office. And, in 1981, to mark the tragic demise of Egyptian President Anwar Sadat, who stayed in The Waldorf whenever in New York City. When Mrs. Sadat learned of this she sent a very touching thank you letter to The Waldorf command.

The ensign of all Hilton Hotels was lowered January 4, 1979, to mark the passing of the global system's founder, Conrad N. Hilton.

The task of determining which ensigns shall be displayed, and in what order, is neither an easy nor a casual decision. There have been frantic days when flags were raised and lowered like signal bunting in a U.S. Navy convoy. One day recently there were four changes of colors on the poles—honoring Israel, Japan, the British Pilgrims in America and Japan, a second time.

Sometimes the elements snafu the flagstaff operation. A number of times hurricane winds whipped the flags around the poles with such force, that the flags could not be lowered. In these critical situations, friendly neighborhood firemen came to the rescue in the wee hours without sirens or bells.

In command of flag duty are two Waldorf veterans, who have served the hotel for more than three decades each. And each wears two hats. Peter Zlatar, manager of The Towers, is also chief of protocol. It is he who decides which flags are hoisted and where. His in-

The late Lord Mountbatten reviews a group of the Radio City Music Hall's "Rockettes" before a Waldorf performance (PHOTO: BILL MARK).

structions are relegated a day in advance to Louis McElwain, The Waldorf flag master, who is also custodian of furniture. Incidentally, The Waldorf registers employees who have to do with furniture in New York University courses on furniture and antiques to acquaint them with the importance of their responsibilities.

In his latter capacity, McElwain often works 14-hour days supervising the setting up of rooms for conventions and exhibits. In one typical round of the clock he saw to the removal of beds and minor furnishings from 85 rooms to make way for exhibits of thousands of apothecary supplies during a pharmaceutical convention. At the same time he had to strip six rooms in another section for a Japanese festival and then clear sixteen rooms for "rehabilitation" on another floor. He stayed in the hotel overnight for that assignment. Sometimes, he says, he manages to get home for a weekend with his family.

Despite their preoccupation with their alternate roles, both Zlatar and McElwain exhibit extreme pride in being endowed with the care and maintenance of The Waldorf flag tradition. In fact, all of The Waldorf family are warmed by the sight of their flags fluttering in the breeze.

"First thing in the morning, before I come in the employees' entrance, I walk around the block to see what flags are flying," a day maid reveals. "It lets me know who's in the house. And it gives me a feeling all's right in the world. My world."

The Waldorf flag ceremony preceded the Hilton takeover. But no one endorsed or revered the custom more than the late chairman of the hotel. Conrad Hilton was one of the two most patriotic Americans I have ever known. The other was Ike Eisenhower. And I happened to be with both of them on a golf club course one day when Hilton turned to then President Eisenhower and asked, curiously, "In a few words, Ike, for what would you most like to be remembered?"

Without a second's hesitation, Eisenhower answered, "I loved my country."

Hilton nodded thoughtfully. It was obviously a thought he also cherished.

Worlds apart in many ways, the two men really had a lot in common. Despite their lofty attainments in life, neither was snobbish, aloof nor pretentious. Both were unashamedly religious without being overbearingly pious. And neither was embarrassed by an abiding love of his country—and his country's flag.

Connie's devotion was continued by Barron during this nation's bicentennial celebration. Throughout the calendar year of 1976, a flag ceremony, complete with fife and drum, took place twice daily in The Waldorf-Astoria lobby and in every Hilton Hotel across the nation.

It commemorated the 200th anniversary of the founding of our nation. And it gave guests and staff and passers-through a pause in the day's occupation, a moment to reflect on the bounties of democracy and the splendor of Old Glory.

It was just one more dramatic innovation in the elegant Waldorf tradition.

The Concierge Can Do It

THE TELEPHONE RANG IN A small office at the entrance of The Waldorf Towers. It was quickly answered. "Concierge . . . Good morning. May I help you? . . . Yes, sir. Twenty-seven cases of dry-roasted nuts? Yes, sir, I understand. You want me to bring these twenty-seven cases to your plane at Teterboro Airport before seven o'clock? Yes, sir. Yes, I'll take care of it."

"Concierge" is a French word meaning "caretaker." Interestingly, its original derivation is from the Latin: *conservus*, meaning "fellow slave." Today, the concierge is usually found near the front door of a hotel, ready to take care of every guest and serve his every need, however minor or bizarre. The Waldorf-Astoria's concierge is a constantly busy, tall, well-built gentleman who speaks and moves softly and quickly.

On this particular day, the concierge wrote down the patron's urgent request for dry-roasted nuts and glanced at the clock. It was

4:30 p.m. His work shift was due to end at 5 p.m. No way. Nine supermarkets and a trip across the George Washington Bridge later, he had accomplished his "nutty" mission. At Teterboro, he checked his watch—just seconds away from the appointed hour of seven p.m.

Elsewhere in the world there are probably as many concierges as there are bell captains. In our entire country, however, there are no more than five dozen. The select sixty belong to an exclusive concierge fraternity, labeled The Society of the Golden Keys of the United States. And the lapels of their uniform jackets all sport a pair of crossed golden keys.

Nowhere in all hoteldom is there a concierge who served more illustrious guests in more diverse ways than the man who occupies the post at The Waldorf Towers. As a daily routine, the concierge arranges air and rail travel, procures theater tickets, opera seats, baseball, basketball, football and rock concert tickets. Once, The Waldorf's concierge filled a guest's order for six blue ribbon seats in a Mexican bullfight arena!

During a recent stay at the hotel, Jordan's King Hussein discovered his wardrobe was down to its last clean royal shirt. It was 4 p.m. Friday afternoon; he had to catch a plane at noon the next day. Where could he get his shirts laundered and returned in such a short time—on a weekend no less?

So the King phoned the trusty concierge and explained his predicament. "Yes, sir, I understand your emergency," the concierge responded. "We'll have it done."

The King's aide arrived with the four dirty shirts. And the concierge shrugged. Again, he would miss his train to his Long Island home. He would also have to return to the hotel with the finished laundry on his day off. That is, if he could find a laundry to oblige him with overnight service.

He set out with his bundle of shirts and started walking east and north. About a mile away, he located a laundryman willing to do a rush job with generous encouragement.

King Hussein of Jordan arrives at The Waldorf (PHOTO: WILL WEISSBERG).

A much simpler task was assigned the concierge by Nancy Reagan. The First Lady and President Ronald Reagan were departing from the hotel, on their way to the airport, when Nancy paused to hand the concierge a pair of cowboy boots. She asked that would he, please, hold them for safekeeping; their son would stop by later to fetch them.

But Mrs. Douglas MacArthur (a favorite permanent resident) made a trickier appeal for help. She explained to the concierge that she had lost the private telephone number of former President Richard Nixon, who resided in an east side town house at the time. Could he, please, get it for her?

He did. In very short order. But it was a roundabout trail. First, he recalled the name of the Secret Service agent who is frequently assigned to The Towers entrance as security for State Department guests. He contacted the man at Secret Service headquarters downtown and asked him to relay the unlisted number to Mrs. MacArthur.

A guest from South America posed a different kind of problem. Explaining that unforeseen business complications would prevent him from leaving his suite that evening, he asked that the concierge pick up his daughter, who was arriving on a six-thirty p.m. flight from Brazil.

He authorized the concierge to hire a limousine, proceed to Kennedy Airport, greet his daughter, appraise her of the situation, then shepherd her and her luggage to LaGuardia Airport and put her aboard the shuttle flight to Washington.

Again, no sooner said than done—and again late for dinner on Long Island.

Sometimes the assignments come from abroad. A Waldorf resident once missed her plane connections in France. Realizing she would now be unable to attend a dear friend's birthday party scheduled for that night at the Tavern-on-the-Green in New York's Central Park, she considered various ways of expressing her regret.

Finally, she placed an overseas call to The

Waldorf concierge. He cheerily hummed assent, then attended to the chores of selecting an appropriate birthday card, penning the message dictated by the stranded guest, attaching it to a magnum of Dom Perignon and delivering it for presentation to the celebrant that evening.

Most commonly, the concierge is called upon to plot tours for guests unfamiliar with the city, suggest shops stocked with unusual wares and recommend dining places.

Of course, he begins with the hotel's own Peacock Alley, the Bull and Bear, Oscar's, and Inagiku (the finest, most authentic Japanese restaurant this side of Honshu). Room service, he can add, is the equivalent of an elite private caterer. Then there is the Marco Polo, an excellent dining room, but restricted to members only. However, the concierge can provide the hotel guest with a Marco Polo Club membership list and, if the guest finds a member he knows, he should be able to make a phone call and arrange for privileges.

If a guest is in the mood for a meal outside the hotel, as a change of pace, the concierge will first determine the type of food, atmosphere and price range desired. He will then, of course, make the reservations be it public domain or private club.

Then there is the oblique situation in which a popular restaurant adamantly refuses to accept reservations, preferring to operate on a first-come line-up-at-the-rope or wait-at-the-bar system. In this prevalent holding-pattern format, the cagey concierge will arrive early (usually minutes after his five p.m. shift is finished), greet the maitre d' (whom he usually knows) with an eloquently remunerative handshake and take his place at an open table (for four, five, six or more).

Sitting at the table, slowly sipping a tall drink, the lingering occupant does not rouse the ire of other prospective diners patiently waiting at the bar. When the hotel guests do arrive, maybe an hour or two later, they are immediately ushered to the table held by the concierge-in-waiting. After a brief exchange of polite chatter, the concierge will quietly make his exit. And finally head for home.

The concierge in a sense punctuates the hotel's policy of pleasing the guest. And sometimes the guest expresses his pleasure with the caretaker other than in the customary mode.

Once, an Italian diplomat was so impressed with the concierge's manner of speech and aristocratic bearing that he asked him to assume a rather ceremonial role. The diplomat explained he would be entertaining some 150 people at a posh reception in one of The Waldorf's private dining rooms and he would consider it a boon if the concierge stood at the entrance and loudly announced the names of his guests as they arrived for the party.

So it goes. Day in, day out, over the years: "Please find me a gypsy fortune-teller to read palms at my party." . . . "Please telephone your concierge friend at the George V in Paris and have him send a bouquet of spring flowers to the suite of Brooke Shields, with love and kisses from me." . . . "Please make a call to your concierge friend at the Excelsior in Rome and ask him to give me the VIP treatment when I arrive Wednesday . . ."

The requests rarely cause a ripple of disdain or dismay.

What does surprise The Waldorf's can-do concierge, however, is that nobody asked him to wangle an invitation to the wedding of Prince Charles and Lady Diana two days before the ceremony in St. Paul's.

Could it have been managed? Well, the strength of the ties that bind the global concierge fraternity wasn't tested on that feat.

But, we're willing to wager . . .

Foreign Flavor
and Favors

THERE IS NO SUCH THING as a stranger in the land at The Waldorf-Astoria.

Among its staff of 1,800 there is always someone who speaks the stranger's language and who can ease his stay. Some 61 different languages and dialects are listed in the hotel's international directory with the names and locations of employees conversant in Swahili, Swedish, Chinese, Japanese, Indian, Russian, Greek, Portuguese, Arabic, Hebrew, etc., etc.

There are pages and pages for those fluent in French, Spanish, Italian and German. But there are also instant interpreters for Armenians, Croatians, Ethiopians, Hungarians, Iranians, Koreans, Romanians, Yugoslavians and Vietnamese.

All over the hotel, from the back of the house to the front office, upstairs and downstairs, there is some member of the staff wearing a pin in his lapel engraved with the flag of the country whose language he speaks.

The pin is often cause for warm embraces and fraternal greetings from those who recognize a familiar sign connoting inextricable ties that bind.

For many years, The Waldorf was unique in that it had a full-scale overseas department to cater to the needs of its many visitors from abroad.

It even tried to set aside special space for large groups of foreign guests who spoke the same language, with everything from brochures and laundry lists to chambermaids and room service menus, all provided in the visitor's tongue. And even the telephone greeting had a native ring!

So it came to pass that a tardy gentleman who missed his train connections needed a room for another night. The clerk consulted his file and frowned. There was only one room available. "It's one of those set aside for . . ." he started to explain.

But the man interrupted, "Don't tell me about it. Just put me there." The clerk shrugged. And handed him the key.

In the morning, the man reached for the phone to order breakfast. *"Buenos dias,"* sang a cherry voice.

He dropped the phone. *"Buenos dias!?"* What had happened to him yesterday?

Glancing around the room, he saw the checkout notice, which began *"Hora de Salida . . ."*

He opened the door and found a Spanish language newspaper on the floor.

"Where am I?" he cried out frantically.

A chambermaid on her rounds paused to explain that senor was on the eleventh floor, reserved for Spanish, Portuguese and South American guests.

With the advent of jet flights, electronic pictures and satellite communication, the world narrowed and its population grew more sophisticated. Management discovered their overseas guests preferred to mix with the mainstream.

So, after two decades, the foreign floors were eliminated and the overseas department reduced to an international service desk in the lobby. The hotel will reserve a floor of rooms for a foreign group when requested. And there is still a foreign service department to deal with missions, consulates and reservations. But the international desk serves the individual guest from abroad in personal and distinctive ways.

"We do everything from telephone interpretation to making restaurant, theater and airline reservations," a supervisor described. "Whatever their problems—more beds, more towels, if they need a doctor or medicine, or a telegram translated—we do it."

The international desk sends notes to its international arrivals, welcoming them and advising them that a multilingual friend is in the lobby.

"It's a personal touch, makes them feel at home. We get to know them and they get to know us. And when they return, they get so excited, it's hugs and kisses all around."

The desk keeps a tally of daily inquiries. Most are in the category of shopping and gift buying. Some are simple: "A guest calls from outside. She's in a store and the salesclerk doesn't understand her. She puts the clerk on the phone and we translate what the customer wants."

Some are a little more involved: "Two Germans wanted a large American flag like the one at our Park Avenue entrance. We found it somewhere in the Village."

And a few are quite complex: "Some people from South America wanted scientific supplies. Specifically, they wanted a portable optical pyrometer, an instrument for measuring temperature. But it had to be for a certain intensity of temperature. I called around and finally found a supply company in New Jersey. But it took a lot of persuasion to get them to deliver it."

At this point, the supervisor was approached by a distinguished gray-haired gentleman who hesitated, "S'il vous plait . . .?" He paused.

"Parlez francais? Oui," the woman smiled.

They went on then at great length, the language flowing, punctuated with smiles and gestures. Nodding, the supervisor opened her desk drawer and withdrew a well-thumbed directory. She leafed through it, then wrote something down on a piece of paper.

After a brief exchange and more nodding, she handed the man a city map printed in French, plus her pencilled sketch to guide him to his destination. The man bowed, reached over and kissed her hand.

A curious American observer unceremoniously put the question, "What did he want?"

"Oh," she shrugged, "a Kosher delicatessen." And she promptly entered the transaction in her log.

The international cross section of Waldorf visitors is plainly visible in the lobby scene. The air vibrates with the jabber of flavored accents. And the decor is frilled with foreign dress—saris, tunics, caftans, smocks, cassocks, turbans, fezzes and skullcaps.

Foreign travellers have always flocked to The Waldorf-Astoria. Among royalty, it's a case of "one king tells another . . ." Among the citizenry, it's the certainty that The Waldorf will treat them royally, too.

All of the hotel's restaurant and room service menus are available in a myriad of languages. And telephone messages are also multilingual.

Special efforts are made to ensure the foreign visitor's comfort and well-being. And such extra touches as roses with room service for Hindu guests, who traditionally hold a flower in their hands as they chant their morning prayers.

Occasionally, however, the foreign guests try enhancing the special treatment in their own fashion. It can, to say the least, be disconcerting.

There was even the time banquet waiters stood aghast as some fervent Greek patriots unwrapped small cooking utensils and canned heat at the ballroom tables, ready to prepare their own moussaka!

Lost and Found

IF POET JOHN MILTON HAD lost his paradise somewhere in The Waldorf, chances are the hotel would have forwarded it to his home address with a thoughtful note.

Guests have left behind all kinds of items and critters—cats and dogs, goldfish, turtles and birds in gilded cages. Also furs and jewels, jackets and shoes, gowns and robes, wigs and toupees, dentures, spectacles, hearing aids and crutches.

It may be a puzzlement as to how people check in on crutches and leave without them, but it is safe to assume that The Waldorf treatment enables the lame and the halt to walk again.

Nevertheless, the lost and found department is a small, but significant, example of the extremes The Waldorf will go to in ministering to its guests, including the absent-minded.

Another Waldorf first, and one of few in operation, lost and found over the years has returned slippers to Eddie Cantor, underwear to Lowell Thomas, a pair of cameras to the Ethiopian Embassy, five shirts to an Indian potentate, a cigarette holder to a man in Rio de Janeiro, a straw hat to the wife of a French ambassador, eyeglasses to the finance minister of China and photos left behind by the ambassador of Norway.

Then there was the salesman from Cleveland, Ohio, who sent this communication: "When checking out of Suite A this morning, I left behind the better part of a bottle of good old Johnnie Walker in its original gift box. I would consider it a miracle if it were turned in, but would appreciate it just the same if you would inquire. Please be assured that I do not expect to be so fortunate as to have you locate the package."

Well, Lost and Found not only located the better part of his good old booze, but it also carefully wrapped it and sent the "miracle" to the salesman's Cleveland address.

Items left behind at The Waldorf could easily fill an attic or a basement. The annual tally of from five to eight thousand articles could supply a year's inventory for a variety store.

Instead, the assortment—from a tiny tie stud to a steamer trunk—is stashed on shelves, in drawers, file cabinets, barrels, bins and corners of a room no bigger than a pantry in one of The Tower suites.

For some obscure reason, lost and found has long been managed by ladies of delicate dimensions and Irish descent. For twenty-three years, it was the bailiwick of Roslyn Muldoon, a short, slight colleen, who collected and dispatched an infinite array of strayed treasures, tidbits and trivia. When she retired, the keys of the kingdom were passed to Mary O'Flaherty, formerly a hotel cashier, who demonstrated the same perspicacity as her predecessor for detail and Scotland Yard sleuthing.

In a mere 13 by 21 feet of space, bulging with bundles, cartons and files, there is barely room for Mary O'Flaherty, which may be why she remains as slim and lithe as the day she joined The Waldorf family more than two decades ago.

She scoots about from her squat steel desk to an old upright typewriter on a small table, to the telephone that buzzes imploringly. And hearkens to the plaintive cries of "Did you happen to find?" or "Oh, say did you see . . .my diary, my slippers, my pipe rack, my daughter's doll . . .?"

At first glance, the room is a mess! But the logs and files actually are in impeccable order. And Mrs. O'Flaherty can quickly put her hand on the item of inquiry.

When Gregory Peck called to say he lost his X-rays and wondered, perhaps, if he left them in his hotel suite, Mrs. O'Flaherty could assure him that they had, indeed, been turned in and they would be mailed to him immediately.

That same day she could respond similarly to a caller from New Zealand who left her shoes, a man from Paris who missed his robe and a fretful mother in California who itemized her youngsters' leftovers in room 895 as including one green sweater, two white shirts, a pair of tan short pants and assorted boys' underwear.

Lost and found gets calls from all over the globe. And the hotel annually posts thousands of packages to dozens of different countries.

In the case of valuables (jewelry, cameras, wallets), contact is made immediately, with discretion. The person notified is simply informed, "Jewelry was found in your room." A detailed description is then required. If the valuables are not claimed within fifteen days, they are sent to the New York City Police Lost Property Department.

Sometimes the route of lost and found gets a bit tangled. Not long ago, a gentleman from Norway left The Waldorf-Astoria and took a train for Boston. That afternoon, the manager of the Tremont Hotel in Boston called Mrs. O'Flaherty advising her that a Mr. Hansen left some clothes behind in The Waldorf and would she be so kind as to forward them to his next destination, the Queen Elizabeth Hotel in Toronto, Canada. The instructions were to send the package via Federal Express and charge it to the gentleman's American Express card.

Twelve days later, Mary was surprised to hear from Federal Express that the gentleman in question never registered at the Canadian hotel and they were awaiting further instructions. So she called the manager of the Tremont, who coolly responded he had nothing to do with the matter but had merely delivered the guest's requests. The package was eventually returned to The Waldorf. And Mrs. O'Flaherty sat down at her ancient typewriter and addressed a letter to Norway. "I wrote to tell him his clothes were being held here for safekeeping."

And back came a letter of reply: "I am thankful that you have take care of my clothes which I forget at my room in Your hotel when I leave You on the morning of May 18 . . ." He then asked that the package be sent to "my private address in Norway." After a seven-weeks cycle, the clothes and their owner were reunited. And another grateful guest was duly impressed.

Tucked away in her cubbyhole quarters, separated by a specially constructed Dutch door ("So people can't barge in, spot an umbrella and claim it as theirs . . ."), the caretaker of lost and found busily packs a pile of sundries in plastic bags, numbering each with a black marker, and stores them in convenient places.

It's a familiar format: Each item is logged by number, noting the date received, the time, the room number, the occupants, the date the guests checked out and by whom the item was turned in.

The day's return is laden with appliances—hair dryers, alarm clocks, water picks, electric rollers, electric shaving gear—and the usual load of spectacles.

Beneath the desk are boxes of eyeglasses and eyeglass cases, long unclaimed. "Whenever a staffer forgets his specs, he knows where to come," Mrs. O'Flaherty says with a grin. "We'll fit him properly, lend him a pair; but he'll have to return them when he goes off duty."

The guardian of lost and found often worries about items of obvious sentiment. There is a picture of two children in a handsome silver frame. The owner was notified. "The woman said she would pick it up, but she hasn't come around yet," Mrs. O'Flaherty sighed. "I hope she's all right, I'll call her again."

Also tucked away is a sketch pad with pages of drawings. "They're so beautiful, you would think the artist would want them."

A grandmother herself, she keeps a particularly watchful eye on a box of furred strays. "Oh, the stuffed animals, they get caught up in the sheets, go down the linen chutes . . . A man from Sweden wrote recently asking if a teddy bear was found in his room. 'My little boy sleeps with it,' he said. Luckily, it was retrieved from the chute. It was old and tattered, must have got a lot of cuddling. We sent it along."

The department, like the hotel, reflects the seasons. After the summer's lull comes the crescendo of fall social events.

When the banquets begin, the earrings come rolling in, mostly singles, seldom in pairs; also the tie pins, clasps and cuff links.

In the winter, coats and jackets, furred and cloth, fill the racks of lost and found. Mostly, they're from Sir Harry's Bar. Sir Harry's is the largest single source of lost items. Maybe it's the dimness of the setting, the overindulgence of the imbiber, or the easy transit from exit to taxicab that enables a patron to forget his outer garment.

Which brings up another axiom supported by the annals of lost and found: Men are more forgetful than women. Certainly, women seldom lose their coats. What they do lose is shoes. The twentieth floor depository is a veritable stockroom of shoes. Shoes in boxes, shoes loose, single shoes, shoes in pairs—left in the closet, the bathroom, on chairs, but mostly under the bed.

Categorically, the rooms produce clothes and the ballrooms jewelry; the lobby is clearly the area for lost address books and wallets, attaché cases and cameras, as well as tapes and cassettes carelessly dropped or mislaid.

One lone golf club was once left on an elevator. It stands in a corner wastebasket waiting to be claimed.

And, for a long time, a pair of skis in a zippered carrying case rested alongside.

The skis were turned in by a garage man on a February afternoon. He reported they belonged to a Mr. Kennedy who had left them saying he would return the next day. Files showed a Mr. Kennedy checked out of the hotel on February 19th. He was contacted, but said they weren't his.

So they stood in the corner bin through the winter and spring. "They took up no room," Mrs. O'Flaherty shrugged. "But I wondered why they weren't claimed."

Then, on August 19th, a Mr. Jenkins stood at the threshold of the half-door and reported he lost a pair of skis some months ago.

"Months ago?" Mrs. O'Flaherty shook her head.

The man spotted the skis in the basket and pointed: "They're mine."

"How do I know?" Mrs. O'Flaherty responded.

"There's a tag inside with the name Jenkins."

Sure enough, it was there. Who was Kennedy? A girl he was visiting in the hotel at the time. Jenkins wasn't even a guest.

And why the delay in claiming the expensive slopes equipment?

He shrugged. He had been traveling. After that, he had no need for them. And besides, he nodded, he knew they would be safe at The Waldorf.

Happy New Year, America

DESPITE HIS YOUTH, DONNY OSMOND was already a superstar in two worlds of entertainment in 1981—television and recordings.

Donny Osmond was also the beneficiary of dazzling headlines because of the news that he was in rehearsal for his debut on Broadway in the world of musical comedy. He was about to star in a revival of the late George M. Cohan's 1904 hit, "Little Johnny Jones."

In the raw estimate of show biz, Donny Osmond was hot. But was he ready for the big international job of hosting New Year's Eve at The Waldorf?

For months The Waldorf and CBS had been studying the versatile talents and universal appeal of this "All-American Boy" in greasepaint. After a respectable mourning period for its traditional New Year's host, Guy Lombardo, The Waldorf had decided to change gears and come up with a new and different kind of commitment. With its well-

Donny Osmond is the featured performer at a Waldorf New Year's Eve celebration to greet 1982.

recognized ability to make changes that would keep the hotel abreast of and often ahead of trends, Donny Osmond was signed as master of ceremonies and top star of The Waldorf-Astoria's globally famed year end gala, which was titled "Happy New Year, America."

A few minutes after the fun started at nine o'clock on New Year's Eve, Donny jumped off the stage onto the ballroom floor with a cordless mike, moving among the crowd, personally introducing himself to the dancing guests—and, over the air, introducing the guests to all and sundry.

Backing up Donny Osmond was the music of the firmly entrenched younger celebrity in the orchestra world, Peter Duchin, who is music director of The Waldorf. Duchin had two bands on deck, alternating. There was never a moment all night when guests were without dance music, except during showtimes.

Sharing the spotlight with Donny in the singing department was Marilyn McCoo, one of the year's most beautiful and most talented voices.

In corners of the ballroom, visible to all, were giant TV screens on which local and "imported" entertainment were presented. Highlights of the fun in The Las Vegas Hilton and Jilly's in Texas provided lively segments. Waldorf revelers were even treated to a close-up of WMCA's Big Apple descending in Times Square at the stoke of twelve.

It was the most sparkling and happiest New Year's Eve The Waldorf has known in recent years. It was also a most pleasing conclusion to 1981—to have Donny Osmond break the late Guy Lombardo's record for filling the ballroom.

The ballroom was not the only scene of jammed merriment in The Waldorf that night. Sir Harry's Bar got so heavily populated that guests had to be invited to take their drinks out into the lobby in order to abide by fire regulations. The Hideaway had the same over-

flow situation. Peacock Alley, as expected, had to turn away countless couples.

The Bull and Bear Restaurant downstairs on the street level corner of East 49th Street was booming. It looked as if it were thronged wall to wall with black ties. In fact, halfway through the evening Bob Whalen, the manager, found it necessary to change from black tie to a fireman's red bow so that guests could identify who was in charge. With a musical group going full blast, the Bull and Bear was reminiscent of legendary New Year's parties of yesteryear in El Morocco and the 21 Club. At three in the morning, Whalen found it difficult to persuade the happy mob that the party was over.

On New Year's Day, at four in the afternoon, while I was undergoing some liquid resuscitation in a midtown recovery room with a couple of hotel exec friends, I gave them a run-through of my night on the town inside "The Greatest of Them All" with details about Donny Osmond's box office appeal. They shook their heads.

One of them, John Mados, owner and managing director of the Wyndham Hotel, concluded: "Somebody in The Waldorf must be doing something right."

The other, Neal Lang, retired former general manager of The Plaza, nodded and submitted: "Correction! Everybody in The Waldorf seems to be doing something right."